Learning Django 5

Program web apps with complete django capabilities, ORM, Template, MongoDB and Docker containerization

Clara Stein

Published by: GitforGits

Publisher: Sonal Dhandre

www.gitforgits.com

support@gitforgits.com

Printed in India

First Printing: June 2024

ISBN: 9788119177820

Cover Design by: Kitten Publishing

Prologue

It is with much pleasure that I greet you and invite you to "Learning Django 5"; my name is Clara Stein. This book is intended for seasoned Python programmers, web developers looking to expand their skill set, and newcomers eager to dive into the world of web development. In this book, I will demystify Django 5 and demonstrate how to use this powerful framework to create robust, scalable web applications with ease and efficiency. Django's simplicity and power have captivated me since the moment I discovered it. Django's "batteries-included" philosophy means that it ships with many tools and features out of the box, allowing developers to focus on writing code rather than reinventing the wheel. With Django 5, the framework has become even more powerful and user-friendly, making it ideal for creating modern web applications.

We begin our journey by installing Django on a Linux system. I'll walk you through the installation process, configure virtual environments, and create your first Django project. Our sample application, BookTech, will be our constant companion throughout the book, giving us a real-world context in which to apply what we've learned. This hands-on approach allows you to immediately see the practical applications of each concept.

Understanding the fundamentals of Django is critical, so we'll begin by delving into Django models and ORM. You'll learn how to define models, perform database migrations, and work with the ORM to achieve efficient data querying. These skills are the foundation of any Django application, allowing you to handle data with confidence and precision. As we progress, you'll learn about the power of Django views and URL routing. We will look at both function-based and class-based views, giving you the freedom to choose the best approach for your projects. Mapping URLs to views and managing forms within views will become second nature to you, allowing you to create dynamic, responsive web applications.

Templates are the foundation of any web application's front end, and I'll demonstrate how to create and customize them effectively. From basic template creation to advanced techniques such as template inheritance and custom tags, you will learn how to render dynamic content beautifully and efficiently. User authentication and authorization are critical components of any application, and Django excels at these tasks. We will implement secure user registration, login, and permission management to make your applications both user-friendly and secure. You'll also learn how to customize the default user model to meet your specific requirements.

We'll discuss SEO and visibility strategies to help your application stand out in a crowded web landscape. You'll learn how to create site maps, configure RSS feeds, and use SEO best practices to boost your site's search engine ranking and user engagement. Deployment and scaling can be daunting tasks, but I'll walk you through them step by step. You'll learn how to use Docker to containerize your application, deploy it to AWS, and configure Jenkins for continuous integration and deployment pipelines. These skills are essential for ensuring consistent and dependable deployments in production environments.

Finally, maintaining and monitoring your application is critical to its long-term success. We'll use tools like Amazon CloudWatch, New Relic, and Sentry to track performance and errors, ensuring that your application runs smoothly and efficiently.

"Learning Django 5" is more than just a technical reference; it takes you on an educational trip through the heart of Django web development. My goal is to give you the knowledge and confidence to create exceptional web applications. So, let's get started and make your ideas a reality with Django 5.

Content

Preface

"Learning Django 5" is intended to help Python programmers, aspiring full stack developers, and web developers build robust and scalable web applications quickly and efficiently. with a basic understanding of Python scripting. Hands-on labs and interactive tasks are used throughout the book to help you practice and apply the concepts as you learn.

Beginning with a thorough introduction to Django 5, you'll learn how to install and configure Django on a Linux server, set up virtual environments, and create your first Django project, BookTech. The book walks you through the fundamentals of Django models and ORM, teaching you how to define models, perform database migrations, and interact with the ORM to optimize data querying. You will learn about Django views, including function-based and class-based views, URL mapping, and form handling. The templates section will show you how to create and inherit templates, use template tags and filters, and pass data to templates for dynamic rendering.

Advanced topics are thoroughly covered, including user authentication, permission management, and extending the default user model. You'll also learn how to use essential features like site maps, RSS feeds, and SEO optimization to boost your app's visibility and user engagement. The book then goes over deployment and scaling, teaching you how to containerize your application with Docker, deploy to cloud platforms like AWS, and set up continuous integration and deployment pipelines in Jenkins. You will learn how to maintain and monitor your application with tools such as Amazon CloudWatch, New Relic, and Sentry, ensuring that it runs smoothly in production.

In this book you will learn how to:

- Comprehensive Django setup with step-by-step installation and configuration of Django 5.
- Mastering models and ORM to define models and interact with databases efficiently.
- Understand and implement both function-based and class-based views seamlessly.
- Perform dynamic template rendering wherein you create, inherit, and customize templates for dynamic web content.
- Achieve robust user authentication by implementing secure user registration, login, and permission management.
- Learn SEO skills to optimize your site for search engines with site maps and SEO best practices.
- Up and running with docker and containerization to containerize your apps for consistent deployment across environments.
- Learn to deploy applications on AWS with detailed, practical walkthrough.

- Set up and configure Jenkins pipelines for automated testing and deployment.
- Use tools like CloudWatch and Sentry for application performance and error tracking.

GitforGits

Prerequisites

Anyone interested in learning how to build scalable and robust web applications rapidly and efficiently would benefit from reading this book, whether they are existing or aspiring Python programmers, full stack developers, or web developers of any experience level.

Codes Usage

Are you in need of some helpful code examples to assist you in your programming and documentation? Look no further! Our book offers a wealth of supplemental material, including code examples and exercises.

Not only is this book here to aid you in getting your job done, but you have our permission to use the example code in your programs and documentation. However, please note that if you are reproducing a significant portion of the code, we do require you to contact us for permission.

But don't worry, using several chunks of code from this book in your program or answering a question by citing our book and quoting example code does not require permission. But if you do choose to give credit, an attribution typically includes the title, author, publisher, and ISBN. For example, "Learning Django 5 by Clara Stein".

If you are unsure whether your intended use of the code examples falls under fair use or the permissions outlined above, please do not hesitate to reach out to us at support@gitforgits.com.

We are happy to assist and clarify any concerns.

Acknowledgement

I owe a tremendous debt of gratitude to GitforGits, for their unflagging enthusiasm and wise counsel throughout the entire process of writing this book. Their knowledge and careful editing helped make sure the piece was useful for people of all reading levels and comprehension skills. In addition, I'd like to thank everyone involved in the publishing process for their efforts in making this book a reality. Their efforts, from copyediting to advertising, made the project what it is today.

Finally, I'd like to express my gratitude to everyone who has shown me unconditional love and encouragement throughout my life. Their support was crucial to the completion of this book. I appreciate your help with this endeavour and your continued interest in my career.

Chapter 1: Up and Running with Django 5

Introduction

Welcome to "Up and Running with Django 5." Django is a strong web framework that simplifies the process of creating scalable and reliable web applications. In this chapter, wFirst, we will discover why Django is a great option for building websites, backed by examples that show its features and benefits in action.

Our next step is to show you how to install Linux and configure your development environment. To make sure you can follow along with the installation process, this section includes a detailed walkthrough. An important task for managing dependencies and maintaining project organization is learning how to activate virtual environments. You will learn how to do just that. You will be well-prepared to begin your Django development journey after completing this section.

Now we will jump into making BookTech, your very first Django project. We will show you what's happening during installation and configuration, explaining the project's hierarchy and where everything is located. The learning process will be more engaging and effective with this practical approach, which will give you hands-on experience. Also covered is getting to know the development server and how to launch it, so you can see your code in action right away.

Lastly, this chapter will be concluded with an interactive quiz that will test your knowledge and comprehension of the key concepts mentioned. In a lighthearted and interesting way, this quiz will assess your knowledge and help you retain it.

Welcome to Django

Django 5 marks a significant milestone in the evolution of the Django web framework. Known for its "batteries-included" philosophy, Django provides a comprehensive suite of tools and libraries that make web development both efficient and enjoyable. The latest version, Django 5, brings several enhancements and new features designed to improve performance, security, and developer experience.

Key Features of Django 5

Asynchronous Support

Django 5 continues to enhance its support for asynchronous programming, which is a significant step forward in modern web development. Asynchronous programming allows developers to write non-blocking code using Python's async and await keywords. This feature is particularly useful for applications that require high concurrency, such as chat applications, real-time updates, and live feeds. By supporting asynchronous views, Django 5 enables developers to handle a large number of simultaneous connections efficiently, without the overhead that comes with traditional synchronous views. This means that web applications can be more responsive and scalable, handling more users and operations concurrently without degrading performance. The ability to integrate seamlessly with other asynchronous Python libraries and frameworks further extends Django's capabilities, making it a robust choice for building modern, high-performance web applications.

QuerySet Enhancements

The ORM (Object-Relational Mapping) in Django 5 has received significant improvements, focusing on making database interactions more efficient and expressive. New QuerySet methods and optimizations help developers write more efficient and readable database queries. These enhancements reduce the amount of boilerplate code required and improve the performance of database operations. For example, Django 5 introduces advanced filtering and aggregation methods, allowing developers to perform complex queries with ease. The improved QuerySet API also supports better indexing and caching strategies, which can significantly speed up data retrieval and manipulation. These ORM enhancements make it easier to work with large datasets and complex relational structures, ensuring that applications built with Django 5 are both powerful and efficient.

Enhanced Forms and Views

Django 5 introduces several updates to forms and views, making it easier to handle complex forms and user input. New field types and validation methods provide more flexibility in designing forms that meet specific requirements. These updates include improved support for nested forms, dynamic form generation, and custom validation logic. Additionally, Django 5's view system has been refined to offer better support for asynchronous views, making it possible to process user input and perform backend operations concurrently. This means developers can create more interactive and responsive user interfaces. The enhancements to forms and views simplify the development process, reduce the risk of errors, and enhance the overall user experience.

Improved Security

With each release, Django places a strong emphasis on security, and Django 5 is no exception. This version includes updates to address the latest security threats, ensuring your applications remain safe from vulnerabilities. Django 5 includes built-in protections against common web security issues such as SQL injection, cross-site scripting (XSS), cross-site request forgery (CSRF), and clickjacking. The framework's security middleware has been updated to provide better default settings and easier customization. Additionally, Django 5 includes enhanced support for secure authentication mechanisms, such as OAuth2 and JWT, making it simpler to implement secure user authentication and authorization. By keeping security at the forefront, Django 5 helps developers build applications that protect user data and maintain trust.

Admin Interface Improvements

The Django admin interface is a powerful tool for managing application data, and Django 5 has introduced several usability enhancements to this interface. New customization options allow developers to tailor the admin experience to their needs, making it more intuitive and efficient. Improvements include better support for inline editing, customizable list views, and enhanced filtering and search capabilities. The admin interface's design has also been refined to provide a more modern and user-friendly experience. These enhancements make it easier for administrators to manage complex datasets, streamline workflows, and ensure data integrity.

Support for Newer Python Versions

Django 5 is fully compatible with the latest versions of Python, ensuring developers can leverage the newest features and improvements in the Python language. This compatibility allows developers to take advantage of performance enhancements, new syntax, and additional libraries available in the latest Python releases. By staying up-to-date with Python's development, Django 5 ensures that developers can build applications using the most current and powerful tools available. This forward compatibility also means that applications built with Django 5 will have a longer lifespan and be easier to maintain as the Python ecosystem evolves.

Why Django for Web Development?

Django is a preferred choice for web development for several compelling reasons:

1. Rapid Development: Django's design philosophy is to enable quick development of web applications. With its built-in components, developers can focus on writing application-specific code rather than reinventing the wheel.
2. Scalability: Django is built to handle high-traffic applications. Its architecture supports the scalability needs of large applications, making it suitable for everything from small projects to enterprise-level systems.
3. Security: Django provides robust security features out of the box, protecting against common threats such as SQL injection, cross-site scripting (XSS), and cross-site request forgery (CSRF). The framework's security features are constantly updated to address new vulnerabilities.
4. Versatility: Django is highly versatile and can be used to build a wide range of applications, from content management systems and e-commerce sites to social networks and scientific computing platforms.
5. Community and Ecosystem: Django has a large and active community that contributes to a rich ecosystem of third-party packages and tools. This extensive support network makes it easier to find solutions to common problems and integrate additional functionalities.

Popular Applications built using Django

Instagram

One of the world's most popular social media platforms, Instagram, relies on Django to handle its vast amounts of data and user interactions. Instagram started as a simple photo-sharing app but quickly grew into a massive social media platform with millions of users worldwide. Django's scalability and robust features make it an ideal choice for such a large-scale application. The framework's ORM and built-in admin interface enabled the Instagram team to manage user data and interactions smoothly. Django's ability to scale efficiently allowed Instagram to grow without significant rewrites of its core systems, handling everything from simple photo uploads to complex user interactions.

Pinterest

Another social media giant, Pinterest, uses Django to manage its backend. Pinterest allows users to create and share collections of visual bookmarks, which results in billions of images and user interactions. Django's flexibility and powerful templating engine help Pinterest create a dynamic and engaging user experience. The framework's ORM is essential for managing the vast amount of user-generated content, including images and boards. Django's scalability ensures that Pinterest can handle its growing user base and the increasing volume of content efficiently. By leveraging Django's robust architecture, Pinterest can provide a seamless and responsive service to its users.

Mozilla

The organization behind the Firefox web browser, Mozilla, uses Django for several of its web applications, including the Mozilla Developer Network (MDN). Mozilla values Django's security features and rapid development capabilities, which are critical for maintaining a secure and up-to-date platform for developers worldwide. Django's comprehensive security features, such as protection against SQL injection, cross-site scripting, and cross-site request forgery, ensure that Mozilla's web applications are secure. The framework's rapid development capabilities allow Mozilla to quickly iterate and deploy new features, keeping their applications at the forefront of web technology.

Disqus

A popular commenting system used by many websites, Disqus leverages Django to handle millions of comments and user profiles. Disqus integrates seamlessly into numerous websites, providing a commenting platform that handles a high level of traffic daily. Django's ability to manage large amounts of data and traffic is crucial for Disqus's operations. The framework's robust architecture supports the high level of traffic and ensures data integrity and performance. Django's built-in admin interface allows Disqus to efficiently manage user profiles and comments, providing a smooth experience for both website administrators and users.

The Washington Post

This leading news outlet uses Django for some of its web applications. For a news organization like The Washington Post, managing content efficiently and securely is paramount. Django's content management capabilities allow the publication to deliver news and updates in real-time while ensuring the security of sensitive information. The framework's flexibility and scalability enable The Washington Post to handle a large volume of content and user interactions, providing a reliable and responsive service to you. Django's powerful templating engine helps create engaging and dynamic web pages, enhancing the user experience.

Bitbucket

A web-based version control repository hosting service owned by Atlassian, Bitbucket uses Django to manage its code repositories and user interactions. Bitbucket supports both Git and Mercurial repositories, catering to a wide range of developers. Django's robust ORM and flexibility allow Bitbucket to handle the complex requirements of managing code repositories and user interactions. The framework's scalability ensures that Bitbucket can handle the growing number of repositories and users, providing a seamless experience for developers worldwide.

Prezi

Known for its dynamic and interactive presentation software, Prezi uses Django to handle its complex backend requirements. Prezi allows users to create visually engaging presentations with a zoomable user interface. Django's ability to integrate with various front-end technologies makes it a versatile choice for Prezi. The framework's robust features and flexibility enable Prezi to manage its complex backend requirements, ensuring a smooth and responsive service for its users. Django's scalability ensures that Prezi can handle the increasing number of users and presentations efficiently.

Diving Deeper into Django's Capabilities

Django's robustness lies in its comprehensive framework, which includes:

- Django's admin interface is one of its standout features, allowing developers to manage application data without additional coding. This interface can be customized extensively to fit specific needs.
- Django's ORM is highly intuitive, enabling developers to interact with the database using Python code instead of SQL. This abstraction simplifies database operations and ensures consistency across different database backends.
- Handling forms and user input is straightforward in Django. The framework provides form classes that help with form rendering, validation, and processing, reducing the boilerplate code developers need to write.
- Django's authentication system is built-in, providing user authentication, authorization, and session management out of the box. This system can be extended to include custom user models and authentication mechanisms.
- Middleware in Django allows developers to process requests globally before they reach the view or after the view has processed the request. This is useful for tasks like request

logging, user authentication, and response modification.

- Django's templating engine is powerful and flexible, enabling developers to create dynamic HTML content with ease. The engine supports template inheritance, making it easy to reuse common elements across different pages.
- Django's URL routing system is flexible and powerful, allowing developers to map URLs to views cleanly. This system supports dynamic URLs and regular expression-based routing for complex URL patterns.
- The Django ecosystem includes a vast array of third-party packages that extend the framework's functionality. These packages cover everything from authentication and payment processing to analytics and content management.

It is much easier and faster to construct sophisticated data-driven web applications with the above capabilities. The design of Django encourages reusable components, which helps keep codebases organized and clean.

Setting up Django Environment

Prerequisites for Linux

Before you begin installing Django 5, there are a few prerequisites to ensure your Linux system is ready for the installation:

- Django 5 requires Python 3.8 or higher. Ensure that you have the appropriate version of Python installed.
- pip is the package installer for Python. It allows you to install and manage additional Python packages.
- While not mandatory, using virtual environments is highly recommended. They help in managing dependencies and isolating your project environment.

You can verify the installation of Python and pip by running the following commands in your terminal:

```
python3 --version

pip3 --version
```

If Python or pip is not installed, follow the steps below to install them.

Installing Python

To install Python, follow these steps:

First, update the package list to ensure you have the latest information on the available packages.

```
sudo apt update
```

Install Python using the package manager. For Ubuntu and Debian-based systems, use the following command:

```
sudo apt install python3 python3-pip
```

Check the installation by running:

```
python3 --version

pip3 --version
```

Setting up Virtual Environments

A virtual environment is an isolated environment where you can install Python packages for your project without affecting the global Python installation. This is particularly useful for managing dependencies in your Django projects.

First, install the venv package if it is not already installed.

```
sudo apt install python3-venv
```

Navigate to the directory where you want to create your Django project and create a virtual environment.

```
mkdir ~/BookTech

cd ~/BookTech

python3 -m venv env
```

Activate the virtual environment to start using it.

```
source env/bin/activate
```

Once activated, your terminal prompt will change to indicate that you are working inside the virtual environment.

Installing Django 5

With the prerequisites in place and the virtual environment activated, you can now proceed to install Django 5.

Before installing Django, it's a good idea to upgrade pip to the latest version.

```
pip install --upgrade pip
```

Install Django 5 using pip.

```
pip install django==5.0
```

Confirm that Django has been installed correctly by checking its version.

```
django-admin --version
```

Creating Your First Django 'BookTech' Project

Now that Django is installed, you can create your first Django project, BookTech.

Create a Django Project: Use the django-admin command to create a new Django project.

```
django-admin startproject BookTech
```

Navigate to the Project Directory: Move into the newly created project directory.

```
cd BookTech
```

The startproject command creates a directory structure that includes the project settings and configuration files. Given below is what it looks like:

```
BookTech/
```

```
manage.py
BookTech/
    __init__.py
    settings.py
    urls.py
    asgi.py
    wsgi.py
```

Understanding Project Structure

manage.py

A command-line utility that lets you interact with this Django project. You can use it to start the development server, interact with the database, and more.

BookTech/

This inner directory is the actual Python package for your project.

- init.py: An empty file that tells Python this directory should be considered a Python package.
- settings.py: The settings/configuration for this Django project.
- urls.py: The URL declarations for this Django project; a "table of contents" of your Django-powered site.
- asgi.py: An entry-point for ASGI-compatible web servers to serve your project.
- wsgi.py: An entry-point for WSGI-compatible web servers to serve your project.

Running the Development Server

To see your Django project in action, you need to run the development server.

Start the Development Server: Use the manage.py script to start the server.

```
python manage.py runserver
```

Open your web browser and go to http://127.0.0.1:8000/. You should see the Django welcome page, indicating that your project is up and running.

Troubleshooting Installation Issues

If you encounter any issues during the installation process, following are a few tips to troubleshoot:

- Ensure you are using Python 3.8 or higher. You can check your Python version with python3 --version.
- Make sure your virtual environment is activated. The terminal prompt should indicate that you are in the virtual environment (usually prefixed with (env)).
- If pip cannot find or install a package, try updating pip with pip install --upgrade pip.

With this, you now have Python, pip, and Django installed, and you've created and run your first Django project.

Virtual Environments

Why Virtual Environments?

While setting up the basic development environment and creating your first Django project provides a good starting point, using virtual environments offers significant benefits:

- Different projects may require different versions of the same package. Installing these packages globally can lead to version conflicts.
- Each project may have its own set of dependencies. Keeping these dependencies isolated ensures that changes in one project do not affect another.
- Using virtual environments helps maintain a consistent development environment, which is crucial for deployment and collaboration with other developers.

Creating and Activating Virtual Environments

We will create and activate a virtual environment specifically for our BookTech application.

If you are not already in the BookTech project directory, navigate there.

```
cd ~/BookTech
```

Use the venv module to create a virtual environment. We will name our virtual environment env.

```
python3 -m venv env
```

This command creates a directory named env inside your project directory. This env directory contains the Python executable and a copy of the pip installer, among other things.

After creating the virtual environment, your project directory structure should look like this:

```
BookTech/
    env/
        bin/
        include/
        lib/
        pyvenv.cfg
    manage.py
    BookTech/
        __init__.py
        settings.py
        urls.py
        asgi.py
        wsgi.py
```

To start using the virtual environment, you need to activate it. Activation ensures that the Python interpreter and packages used are isolated within this environment.

```
source env/bin/activate
```

Once activated, your terminal prompt will change to indicate that you are now working inside the virtual environment (usually prefixed with (env)).

With the virtual environment activated, install Django 5. This ensures that Django is installed locally within the virtual environment, not globally.

```
pip install django==5.0
```

Confirm that Django has been installed correctly within the virtual environment by checking its version.

```
django-admin --version
```

Any other Python packages you need for your project should also be installed within the virtual environment. For example, if you need the requests library, you can install it like this:

```
pip install requests
```

When you are done working in the virtual environment, you can deactivate it to return to the global Python environment.

```
deactivate
```

Whenever you start working on your project again, reactivate the virtual environment:

```
source env/bin/activate
```

This configuration lets you manage dependencies and add them without affecting other projects, so you can start developing your Django app with a blank slate. And, while working with virtual environments, you'll notice several benefits that streamline your development process:

- Each project has its own dependencies, preventing conflicts between different projects.
- You can easily manage and upgrade dependencies within a project without worrying about global packages.
- Using virtual environments makes it easier to reproduce your development environment on different machines, ensuring consistency across different setups.
- Isolating project dependencies can also help minimize the risk of dependency-related security vulnerabilities affecting multiple projects.

With your virtual environment set up and Django installed, you are ready to move forward with developing the BookTech application. The next steps involve creating Django apps, defining models, setting up views, and more.

Navigating Files and Directories

Understanding how to navigate and utilize these files is crucial for working with Django effectively.

manage.py

The manage.py script is your go-to tool for managing your Django project. You can use it to run various commands. For instance, to start the development server, navigate to the root of your project directory (where manage.py is located) and run:

```
python manage.py runserver
```

Other useful commands include, creating a new app:

```
python manage.py startapp appname
```

Making and applying migrations:

```
python manage.py makemigrations

python manage.py migrate
```

Creating a superuser:

```
python manage.py createsuperuser
```

settings.py

The settings.py file is where you'll configure various aspects of your Django project. Key sections include:

- INSTALLED_APPS: Lists all the Django applications that are activated in your project.
- MIDDLEWARE: Defines the middleware components that process requests and responses.
- DATABASES: Configures the database settings. By default, it is set to use SQLite.
- TEMPLATES: Configures template engines and directories.
- STATIC_URL: Defines the URL for serving static files.

Following is the sample snippet from settings.py:

```
INSTALLED_APPS = [
    'django.contrib.admin',
    'django.contrib.auth',
    'django.contrib.contenttypes',
    'django.contrib.sessions',
    'django.contrib.messages',
    'django.contrib.staticfiles',
    'myapp',  # Your custom app
]

DATABASES = {
    'default': {
        'ENGINE': 'django.db.backends.sqlite3',
        'NAME': BASE_DIR / 'db.sqlite3',
    }
}
```

urls.py

The urls.py file is where you define the URL patterns for your project. Each URL pattern maps a URL path to a view function or class. This is crucial for directing incoming web requests to the appropriate part of your application.

Following is an example of a simple urls.py:

```
from django.contrib import admin
from django.urls import path, include


urlpatterns = [
    path('admin/', admin.site.urls),
    path('myapp/', include('myapp.urls')),  # Include
URLs from your app
]
```

asgi.py and wsgi.py

These files are essential for deploying your Django application. While you may not interact with them frequently during development, they are crucial for setting up your application on a production server.

- wsgi.py: Used for deploying your project with WSGI servers like Gunicorn.

```
import os
from django.core.wsgi import get_wsgi_application


os.environ.setdefault('DJANGO_SETTINGS_MODULE',
'BookTech.settings')


application = get_wsgi_application()
```

- asgi.py: Used for deploying your project with ASGI servers, supporting asynchronous applications.

```
import os
```

```
from django.core.asgi import get_asgi_application


os.environ.setdefault('DJANGO_SETTINGS_MODULE',
'BookTech.settings')


application = get_asgi_application()
```

Practicing Navigation and Modifications

We will explore how to make some practical modifications to these files:

Adding a New App

Create a new Django app within your project. Run the following command from the root directory (where manage.py is located):

```
python manage.py startapp library
```

This command creates a new directory named library with the following structure:

```
library/

    __init__.py

    admin.py

    apps.py

    migrations/

        __init__.py

    models.py

    tests.py
```

```
    views.py
```

Registering the App

Add your new app to the INSTALLED_APPS list in settings.py:

```
INSTALLED_APPS = [

    ...

    'library',

]
```

Defining URLs for the App

Create a urls.py file inside the library app directory:

```
touch library/urls.py
```

Edit library/urls.py to define URL patterns for the app:

```
from django.urls import path

from . import views


urlpatterns = [

    path('', views.index, name='index'),

]
```

Include the app's URLs in the project's urls.py:

```
from django.contrib import admin

from django.urls import path, include
```

```
urlpatterns = [
    path('admin/', admin.site.urls),
    path('library/', include('library.urls')),
]
```

Creating a Simple View

Define a simple view in library/views.py:

```
from django.http import HttpResponse


def index(request):
    return HttpResponse("Welcome to the Library!")
```

Running the Server

Start the development server to test your setup:

```
python manage.py runserver
```

Accessing the App

Open your browser and go to http://127.0.0.1:8000/library/. You should see the message "Welcome to the Library!".

To successfully develop with Django, one must be familiar with the many file and directory structures described above, as each one serves a unique purpose in the ecosystem.

Running the Development Server

Overview

The Django development server is a lightweight, built-in server designed to help you develop and test your Django applications locally. It is not intended for production use but provides a convenient way to run your application during development. The development server monitors your project files and automatically reloads the server whenever you make changes, making the development process smoother and more efficient.

Launching the Development Server

To run the development server for the BookTech application, follow these steps:

- Ensure you are in the root directory of your Django project, where the manage.py file is located.

```
cd ~/BookTech/BookTech
```

- If your virtual environment is not already activated, activate it to ensure all dependencies are correctly loaded.

```
source ../env/bin/activate
```

- Use the manage.py script to start the development server. By default, the server runs on http://127.0.0.1:8000/.

```
python manage.py runserver
```

Server Configuration and Customization

While the default settings are suitable for most development needs, you may want to customize the server address or port. Given below is how you can do it:

If you want to run the server on a different port, specify the port number after the runserver command. For example, to run the server on port 8080:

```
python manage.py runserver 8080
```

By default, the development server runs on the local IP address 127.0.0.1 (localhost). If you want to make your development server accessible from other devices on your network, you can bind it to 0.0.0.0, which listens on all available IP addresses:

```
python manage.py runserver 0.0.0.0:8000
```

However, for simplicity and consistency throughout this book, we will stick to the default address 127.0.0.1 and port 8000.

Accessing the Application

Once the development server is running, you can access your Django application in a web browser. Open your browser and navigate to http://127.0.0.1:8000/. You should see the default Django welcome page, which confirms that your server is up and running.

Interacting with Application

As you develop your BookTech application, the development server provides real-time feedback by serving your updated code. For example, if you have set up a view and URL for your library app as learned earlier, you can access it directly:

URL Configuration

Ensure that your urls.py files are correctly set up. The main urls.py in the BookTech directory should include the URLs from the library app:

```
from django.contrib import admin

from django.urls import path, include


urlpatterns = [

    path('admin/', admin.site.urls),

    path('library/', include('library.urls')),

]
```

View Configuration

Ensure that your views.py in the library app is correctly defined. For example:

```
from django.http import HttpResponse


def index(request):
```

```
    return HttpResponse("Welcome to the Library!")
```

Access the View

With the development server running, open your browser and go to: http://127.0.0.1:8000/library/.

You should see the message "Welcome to the Library!".

Development Server Output

While the development server is running, your terminal will display log messages that provide valuable information about the server's status and activity. These messages include:

Server Startup

When the server starts, you'll see a message indicating the server is running and listening on a specific address and port.

```
Watching for file changes with StatReloader

Performing system checks...



System check identified no issues (0 silenced).

June 15, 2024 - 12:34:56

Django version 5.0, using settings 'BookTech.settings'

Starting development server at http://127.0.0.1:8000/

Quit the server with CONTROL-C.
```

Requests Handling

Each time you access a URL in your application, the server logs the request, including the HTTP method (GET, POST, etc.) and the requested URL.

```
[15/Jun/2024 12:35:12] "GET /library/ HTTP/1.1" 200 22
```

To stop the development server, simply press Ctrl+C in the terminal where the server is running. This command stops the server and returns you to the command prompt. Now that you know how to launch and work with the Django development server, you can begin developing and testing your BookTech app in real-time.

Summary

The chapter started off by explaining why Django 5 is the best choice for developing powerful web applications and why its features are extremely important in web development. After installing Python and pip, we learned how to set up a virtual environment to isolate project dependencies and set up the development environment on a Linux system. The steps to build and launch a test environment for our BookTech app were learned, and we were made sure that we knew how to handle project-specific dependencies.

After that, we built BookTech, our first Django project, to look into the default directory structure. Files like manage.py, settings.py, urls.py, asgi.py, and wsgi.py were reviewed for their functions. Thanks to this, we now know exactly what these files do and how they affect the setup and operation of a Django project. After that, we figured out how to move around in these folders and files, what they were for, and how to alter them to suit our project requirements.

Furthermore, we discovered the manage.py runserver command, which allows us to launch the Django development server. We saw the default Django welcome page as the application was accessed through http://127.0.0.1:8000/ in a web browser. Modifying the server's settings, such as its port and address, was also learned in the chapter. In the end, we looked at the output from the development server and how it gives us feedback in real-time, which helps us debug and make our app better.

In this way, we laid the groundwork for creating and testing our Django applications, which will serve us well as we move on to more complex ideas and real-world examples in subsequent chapters.

Test Your Knowledge

1. What is the primary purpose of using a virtual environment in Django development?

a) To speed up the server performance
b) To isolate project dependencies and avoid conflicts
c) To make the project more secure
d) To simplify the coding process

Answer: b) To isolate project dependencies and avoid conflicts

2. Which command is used to create a new Django project named BookTech?

a) django-admin createproject BookTech
b) django-admin newproject BookTech
c) django-admin startproject BookTech
d) django-admin initializeproject BookTech

Answer: c) django-admin startproject BookTech

3. What is the role of the manage.py file in a Django project?

a) It contains the settings for the Django project.
b) It is used to interact with the Django project via command-line utilities.
c) It handles URL routing for the Django project.
d) It configures the WSGI server for the Django project.

Answer: b) It is used to interact with the Django project via command-line utilities.

4. Which file in the Django project directory contains the project's settings and configurations?

a) urls.py
b) views.py
c) settings.py
d) wsgi.py

Answer: c) settings.py

5. How do you activate a virtual environment named env in a Linux system?

a) activate env
b) source env/bin/activate
c) start env
d) python env/activate

Answer: b) source env/bin/activate

6. What command do you use to start the Django development server?

a) python manage.py runserver
b) django-admin startserver
c) python manage.py startserver
d) django-admin runserver

Answer: a) python manage.py runserver

7. Where should you navigate to in your browser to view the default Django welcome page after starting the development server?

a) http://127.0.0.1:8000/admin/
b) http://localhost:8000/welcome/
c) http://127.0.0.1:8000/

d) http://localhost:8000/home/

Answer: c) http://127.0.0.1:8000/

8. Which of the following files would you edit to add a new URL pattern for a Django app named library?

a) manage.py
b) settings.py
c) urls.py
d) views.py

Answer: c) urls.py

9. What command would you use to create a new Django app named library within your project?

a) django-admin startapp library
b) python manage.py startapp library
c) django-admin newapp library
d) python manage.py createapp library

Answer: b) python manage.py startapp library

10. What is the purpose of the __init__.py file in a Django app directory?

a) To configure the app's settings
b) To define URL patterns for the app
c) To initialize the app and treat it as a Python package
d) To handle HTTP requests and responses

Answer: c) To initialize the app and treat it as a Python package

CHAPTER 2: DJANGO MODELS AND ORM

Introduction

In this chapter, you'll learn how to create models that are necessary for structuring and storing data in your Django program. To begin, we create models for the BookTech application by defining different sorts of fields and configuring the database. Next, we will go over database migrations for applying and managing schema changes, in which you'll learn how to construct and apply migrations to keep your database in sync with your models as you develop and update them. We then learn how to interface with the Django ORM to query the database via Python code rather than SQL.

As we advance, we will look at relationships and foreign keys, showing you how to create complicated relational models that mimic real-world data structures. This includes establishing one-to-many and many-to-many linkages among various models. You'll also learn how to add custom methods to your models to enable special behaviors and capabilities that are tailored to your application's needs.

At the end of the chapter, you'll undertake a practical experiment to build and query a book catalog using the BookTech program. This will help you realize the topic further.

Defining Models

What Models Mean in Django?

A model is a Python class that represents a database table. Each attribute of the model corresponds to a column in the table, and each instance of the model represents a row in the table. Models are central to Django's powerful ORM system, which allows developers to interact with the database using Python code rather than writing raw SQL queries. This abstraction simplifies database operations, making it easier to perform complex queries and maintain the database schema.

For the BookTech application, models are crucial because they define the structure of the data we want to store. Since BookTech will manage a catalog of books, we need to define models to represent books and any related entities such as authors, publishers, and genres. These models will help us store, retrieve, and manipulate data efficiently. By defining clear models, we ensure that our database schema aligns with the application's requirements, making it easier to develop and scale the application.

Creating a Model

We will create a basic model for the BookTech application. We will start by defining a Book model that includes attributes such as the title, author, publication date, and ISBN.

Navigate to the BookTech App Directory

Ensure you are in the directory where your Django application is located.

```
cd ~/BookTech/BookTech
```

Create the Library App

If you haven't already created an app within the BookTech project, do so now.

```
python manage.py startapp library
```

Define the Book Model

Open the models.py file in the library app directory and define the Book model.

```
from django.db import models


class Book(models.Model):
    title = models.CharField(max_length=200)
    author = models.CharField(max_length=100)
    publication_date = models.DateField()
    isbn = models.CharField(max_length=13)

    def __str__(self):
        return self.title
```

In the above code,

- title: A CharField with a maximum length of 200 characters.
- author: A CharField with a maximum length of 100 characters.
- publication_date: A DateField to store the publication date.
- isbn: A CharField with a maximum length of 13 characters, representing the ISBN.

Register the Model with the Admin Site

To make the Book model manageable through the Django admin interface, register it in the admin.py file of the library app.

```
from django.contrib import admin

from .models import Book


admin.site.register(Book)
```

Migrate the Database

After defining the model, you need to create and apply the database migrations to update the database schema.

- Create Migrations:

```
python manage.py makemigrations library
```

- Apply Migrations:

```
python manage.py migrate
```

These above commands will generate the necessary SQL statements to create the Book table in the database and then apply them.

You can then inspect the database to ensure that the Book table has been created with the specified columns. Use the Django shell or a database management tool to verify the schema.

Create and Query Book Instances

Use the Django shell to create instances of the Book model and query them.

- Enter the Django Shell:

```
python manage.py shell
```

- Create a Book Instance:

```
from library.models import Book

book1 = Book(title="Django Unchained", author="Quentin
Tarantino", publication_date="2012-12-25",
isbn="9781234567897")

book1.save()
```

- Query the Book Model:

```
books = Book.objects.all()

for book in books:

    print(book.title, book.author)
```

You can define and work with models in the same way as shown above. Our BookTech application's data structure is based on the Book model. If we build on this model and add related models for genres, authors, and publishers, BookTech can have a complete data management system.

Database Migrations

Applying Migrations to the Database

In the previous section, we created a Book model for our BookTech application. We will focus now on applying migrations to update the database schema. Migrations are Django's way of propagating changes you make to your models (like adding a new field or deleting a model) into your database schema.

Generate Migrations

The first step is to generate the migration files. These files contain the SQL statements that will be applied to your database to reflect the changes made to your models.

```
python manage.py makemigrations library
```

This command scans the library app for any changes in the models and creates a migration file in the library/migrations/ directory.

Apply Migrations

Once the migration files are generated, you need to apply them to update the database schema.

```
python manage.py migrate
```

And, this command applies all pending migrations to the database, ensuring that the database schema is up to date with the current state of the models.

Managing Database Schema Changes

As your project evolves, you may need to make changes to your database schema. This can involve adding new fields, modifying existing ones, or even deleting models. We will go through some common scenarios and how to handle them using migrations.

Adding a New Field to a Model

Suppose we want to add a genre field to the Book model to categorize books by genre.

Open library/models.py and add the genre field to the Book model.

```
from django.db import models


class Book(models.Model):

    title = models.CharField(max_length=200)

    author = models.CharField(max_length=100)

    publication_date = models.DateField()

    isbn = models.CharField(max_length=13)

    genre = models.CharField(max_length=50,
default='Unknown')  # New field


    def __str__(self):
```

```
        return self.title
```

Create a migration file for this change.

```
python manage.py makemigrations library
```

Apply the migration to update the database schema.

```
python manage.py migrate
```

Modifying an Existing Field

Suppose we want to change the isbn field to have a maximum length of 17 characters instead of 13.

Update the isbn field in library/models.py.

```
class Book(models.Model):

    title = models.CharField(max_length=200)

    author = models.CharField(max_length=100)

    publication_date = models.DateField()

    isbn = models.CharField(max_length=17)  # Modified
field

    genre = models.CharField(max_length=50,
default='Unknown')


    def __str__(self):

        return self.title
```

Create a migration file for this change.

```
python manage.py makemigrations library
```

Apply the migration to update the database schema.

```
python manage.py migrate
```

Removing a Field

Suppose we decide to remove the genre field from the Book model. Remove the genre field from library/models.py.

```
class Book(models.Model):

    title = models.CharField(max_length=200)

    author = models.CharField(max_length=100)

    publication_date = models.DateField()

    isbn = models.CharField(max_length=17)  # Modified
field


    def __str__(self):

        return self.title
```

Create a migration file for this change.

```
python manage.py makemigrations library
```

Apply the migration to update the database schema.

```
python manage.py migrate
```

Renaming a Field

Suppose we want to rename the author field to author_name in the Book model. Update the field name in library/models.py.

```
class Book(models.Model):

    title = models.CharField(max_length=200)

    author_name = models.CharField(max_length=100)  #
Renamed field

    publication_date = models.DateField()

    isbn = models.CharField(max_length=17)


    def __str__(self):

        return self.title
```

Create a migration file for this change.

```
python manage.py makemigrations library
```

Apply the migration to update the database schema.

```
python manage.py migrate
```

Reverting Migrations

If you need to revert a migration for any reason, you can do so using the migrate command with a specific migration number.

List all migrations to find the specific migration number you want to revert to.

```
python manage.py showmigrations library
```

Revert the database to a specific migration.

```
python manage.py migrate library <migration_number>
```

For example, if you want to revert to the initial migration, you might use:

```
python manage.py migrate library 0001
```

Sample Program: Managing Migration to Model Updates

We will go through a practical example where we make several changes to the Book model and manage the migrations accordingly.

Start with the initial Book model as defined previously.

```
class Book(models.Model):

    title = models.CharField(max_length=200)

    author = models.CharField(max_length=100)

    publication_date = models.DateField()

    isbn = models.CharField(max_length=13)


    def __str__(self):

        return self.title
```

Modify the model to include a genre field.

```
class Book(models.Model):

    title = models.CharField(max_length=200)

    author = models.CharField(max_length=100)

    publication_date = models.DateField()

    isbn = models.CharField(max_length=13)

    genre = models.CharField(max_length=50,
default='Unknown')
```

```
    def __str__(self):
        return self.title
```

Generate and apply migrations.

```
python manage.py makemigrations library
python manage.py migrate
```

Change the isbn field to have a maximum length of 17.

```
class Book(models.Model):
    title = models.CharField(max_length=200)
    author = models.CharField(max_length=100)
    publication_date = models.DateField()
    isbn = models.CharField(max_length=17)
    genre = models.CharField(max_length=50,
default='Unknown')

    def __str__(self):
        return self.title
```

Generate and apply migrations.

```
python manage.py makemigrations library
python manage.py migrate
```

Remove the genre field from the model.

```
class Book(models.Model):
    title = models.CharField(max_length=200)
    author = models.CharField(max_length=100)
    publication_date = models.DateField()
    isbn = models.CharField(max_length=17)

    def __str__(self):
        return self.title
```

Generate and apply migrations.

```
python manage.py makemigrations library
python manage.py migrate
```

Update the field name.

```
class Book(models.Model):
    title = models.CharField(max_length=200)
    author_name = models.CharField(max_length=100)
    publication_date = models.DateField()
    isbn = models.CharField(max_length=17)

    def __str__(self):
```

```
        return self.title
```

Generate and apply migrations.

```
python manage.py makemigrations library

python manage.py migrate
```

If needed, revert to an earlier state.

```
python manage.py showmigrations library

python manage.py migrate library 0002
```

By doing so, the database schema is restored to the condition specified during the second migration. The ability to apply and manage migrations is crucial for efficiently handling schema changes and keeping your database up-to-date with your code.

Interacting with ORM

What is ORM in Django?

ORM, or Object-Relational Mapping, is a programming technique used to convert data between incompatible type systems in object-oriented programming languages. The ORM allows developers to interact with the database using Python code instead of writing SQL queries. This abstraction layer simplifies database operations, making it easier to perform CRUD (Create, Read, Update, Delete) operations and manage database schema changes.

The role of the Django ORM is to provide a high-level interface for interacting with the database. It translates Python code into SQL queries, manages database connections, and handles data retrieval and manipulation. By using the ORM, developers can work with database records as if they were normal Python objects, making the development process more intuitive and less error-prone.

Performing Queries with Django ORM

We will explore how to perform various database operations using the Django ORM. We will use the Book, Author, and Publisher models defined in the previous sections.

Setting up the Environment

Ensure your Django project is set up and the models are defined as follows in library/models.py:

```
from django.db import models
from datetime import date


class Author(models.Model):
    first_name = models.CharField(max_length=50)
    last_name = models.CharField(max_length=50)
    birth_date = models.DateField()

    def __str__(self):
        return f"{self.first_name} {self.last_name}"

    def full_name(self):
        return f"{self.first_name} {self.last_name}"

    def get_books(self):
        return Book.objects.filter(author=self)

class Publisher(models.Model):
    name = models.CharField(max_length=100)
    address = models.CharField(max_length=255)
```

```
    city = models.CharField(max_length=100)

    state_province = models.CharField(max_length=100)

    country = models.CharField(max_length=100)

    website = models.URLField()


    def __str__(self):

        return self.name


    def formatted_address(self):

        return f"{self.address}, {self.city},
{self.state_province}, {self.country}"


class Book(models.Model):

    title = models.CharField(max_length=200)

    author = models.ForeignKey(Author,
on_delete=models.CASCADE)

    publication_date = models.DateField()

    isbn = models.CharField(max_length=17)

    publishers = models.ManyToManyField(Publisher)


    def __str__(self):

        return self.title
```

```
    def book_age(self):
        today = date.today()
        return today.year - self.publication_date.year
```

Entering the Django Shell

Use the Django shell to interact with the database:

```
python manage.py shell
```

Creating Records

Create instances of Author, Publisher, and Book:

```
from library.models import Author, Book, Publisher
from datetime import date


# Create authors
author1 = Author(first_name="John", last_name="Doe",
birth_date="1970-01-01")
author1.save()
author2 = Author(first_name="Jane", last_name="Smith",
birth_date="1980-05-15")
author2.save()


# Create publishers
```

```
publisher1 = Publisher(name="Tech Books Publishing",
address="123 Main St", city="New York",
state_province="NY", country="USA",
website="http://techbooks.com")

publisher1.save()

publisher2 = Publisher(name="Knowledge Hub Publishing",
address="456 Elm St", city="San Francisco",
state_province="CA", country="USA",
website="http://knowledgehub.com")

publisher2.save()


# Create books

book1 = Book(title="Learning Django", author=author1,
publication_date=date(2020, 1, 1), isbn="9781234567890")

book1.save()

book1.publishers.add(publisher1, publisher2)


book2 = Book(title="Advanced Django", author=author2,
publication_date=date(2018, 6, 1), isbn="9781234567891")

book2.save()

book2.publishers.add(publisher1)
```

Retrieving Records

- Retrieve All Books:

```
books = Book.objects.all()
```

```
for book in books:
    print(f"Title: {book.title}, Author: {book.author.full_name()}, Publication Date: {book.publication_date}, ISBN: {book.isbn}")
```

- Retrieve a Single Book:

```
book = Book.objects.get(id=1)
print(f"Title: {book.title}, Author: {book.author.full_name()}")
```

- Filter Books by Author:

```
books_by_author1 = Book.objects.filter(author=author1)
for book in books_by_author1:
    print(f"Title: {book.title}, Publication Date: {book.publication_date}")
```

- Retrieve Books Published by a Specific Publisher:

```
books_by_publisher1 = publisher1.book_set.all()
for book in books_by_publisher1:
    print(f"Title: {book.title}, Author: {book.author.full_name()}")
```

Updating Records

- Update a Book's Title:

```
book = Book.objects.get(id=1)
book.title = "Mastering Django"
```

```
book.save()
```

- Add a New Publisher to a Book:

```
book = Book.objects.get(id=2)

publisher3 = Publisher(name="New Age Publishing",
address="789 Oak St", city="Los Angeles",
state_province="CA", country="USA",
website="http://newagepublishing.com")

publisher3.save()

book.publishers.add(publisher3)
```

Deleting Records

- Delete a Book:

```
book = Book.objects.get(id=2)

book.delete()
```

- Delete an Author:

```
author = Author.objects.get(id=1)

author.delete()
```

Complex Queries

- Retrieve Books Published After a Certain Date:

```
books_published_after_2019 =
Book.objects.filter(publication_date__gt="2019-01-01")

for book in books_published_after_2019:
```

```
    print(f"Title: {book.title}, Publication Date: {book.publication_date}")
```

- Retrieve Authors Who Have Written Books Published by a Specific Publisher:

```
authors_published_by_publisher1 = Author.objects.filter(book__publishers=publisher1).distinct()

for author in authors_published_by_publisher1:

    print(f"Author: {author.full_name()}")
```

- Retrieve Books with a Specific Keyword in the Title:

```
django_books = Book.objects.filter(title__icontains="Django")

for book in django_books:

    print(f"Title: {book.title}, Author: {book.author.full_name()}")
```

Using Custom Methods

- Retrieve Book Ages Using a Custom Method:

```
for book in Book.objects.all():

    print(f"Title: {book.title}, Age: {book.book_age()} years")
```

- Retrieve Full Addresses of Publishers Using a Custom Method:

```
for publisher in Publisher.objects.all():
```

```
    print(f"Publisher: {publisher.name}, Address:
{publisher.formatted_address()}")
```

This method simplifies development, makes code more readable and maintainable, and uses these different queries and interactions with the ORM to efficiently manage and retrieve data in your Django application.

Relationships and Foreign Keys

Understanding Foreign Keys and related Terms

A foreign key is a field in one model that links to a primary key in another model, establishing a relationship between the two models. This is crucial for representing real-world relationships within your database. For example, in our BookTech application, a book may have a relationship with an author, where each book is linked to a specific author.

Important concepts to know:

- Foreign Key: A field that creates a many-to-one relationship between two models. It points to a primary key in another model.
- One-to-Many Relationship: This is represented by a foreign key in Django, where multiple instances of one model can be related to a single instance of another model.
- One-to-One Relationship: A relationship where one instance of a model is related to one instance of another model, represented by a OneToOneField.
- Many-to-Many Relationship: A relationship where multiple instances of one model can be related to multiple instances of another model, represented by a ManyToManyField.

Building a Relational Model

We will build relational models for our BookTech application. We will create two new models: Author and Publisher, and establish relationships between them and the Book model.

Create the Author Model

First, we will define an Author model. Each book will have one author, but an author can write many books (one-to-many relationship).

Open library/models.py and add the Author model:

```
from django.db import models
```

```
class Author(models.Model):

    first_name = models.CharField(max_length=50)

    last_name = models.CharField(max_length=50)

    birth_date = models.DateField()


    def __str__(self):

        return f"{self.first_name} {self.last_name}"
```

Include a Foreign Key to Author

Modify the Book model to include a foreign key to the Author model.

```
class Book(models.Model):

    title = models.CharField(max_length=200)

    author = models.ForeignKey(Author,
on_delete=models.CASCADE)

    publication_date = models.DateField()

    isbn = models.CharField(max_length=17)


    def __str__(self):

        return self.title
```

- author: A ForeignKey field that establishes a many-to-one relationship with the Author model. The on_delete=models.CASCADE argument specifies that when an author is deleted, all related books should also be deleted.

Create the Publisher Model

We will define a Publisher model. A book can have multiple publishers and a publisher can publish multiple books (many-to-many relationship).

Add the Publisher model to library/models.py:

```
class Publisher(models.Model):

    name = models.CharField(max_length=100)

    address = models.CharField(max_length=255)

    city = models.CharField(max_length=100)

    state_province = models.CharField(max_length=100)

    country = models.CharField(max_length=100)

    website = models.URLField()


    def __str__(self):

        return self.name
```

Include a Many-to-Many Relationship with Publisher

Modify the Book model to include a many-to-many relationship with the Publisher model.

```
class Book(models.Model):

    title = models.CharField(max_length=200)

    author = models.ForeignKey(Author,
on_delete=models.CASCADE)

    publication_date = models.DateField()

    isbn = models.CharField(max_length=17)
```

```
    publishers = models.ManyToManyField(Publisher)

    def __str__(self):
        return self.title
```

- publishers: A ManyToManyField that establishes a many-to-many relationship with the Publisher model. This allows a book to be published by multiple publishers and a publisher to publish multiple books.

Create and Apply Migrations

After updating the models, generate and apply the migrations to update the database schema.

- Generate Migrations:

```
python manage.py makemigrations library
```

- Apply Migrations:

```
python manage.py migrate
```

Register the Models with the Admin Site

To manage these models through the Django admin interface, register them in library/admin.py:

```
from django.contrib import admin
from .models import Book, Author, Publisher

admin.site.register(Book)
admin.site.register(Author)
admin.site.register(Publisher)
```

Creating and Querying Related Instances

Use the Django shell to create and query instances of these related models.

- Enter the Django Shell:

```
python manage.py shell
```

- Create Author Instances:

```
from library.models import Author, Book, Publisher

author1 = Author(first_name="John", last_name="Doe",
birth_date="1970-01-01")

author1.save()

author2 = Author(first_name="Jane", last_name="Smith",
birth_date="1980-05-15")

author2.save()
```

- Create Publisher Instances:

```
publisher1 = Publisher(name="Tech Books Publishing",
address="123 Main St", city="New York",
state_province="NY", country="USA",
website="http://techbooks.com")

publisher1.save()

publisher2 = Publisher(name="Knowledge Hub Publishing",
address="456 Elm St", city="San Francisco",
state_province="CA", country="USA",
website="http://knowledgehub.com")

publisher2.save()
```

- Create Book Instances and Associate with Authors and Publishers:

```
book1 = Book(title="Learning Django", author=author1,
publication_date="2023-01-01", isbn="9781234567890")

book1.save()

book1.publishers.add(publisher1, publisher2)


book2 = Book(title="Advanced Django", author=author2,
publication_date="2023-06-01", isbn="9781234567891")

book2.save()

book2.publishers.add(publisher1)
```

- Querying the Models:

```
# Get all books by a specific author

author_books = Book.objects.filter(author=author1)

for book in author_books:

    print(book.title, book.publication_date)


# Get all books published by a specific publisher

publisher_books = publisher1.book_set.all()

for book in publisher_books:

    print(book.title, book.author.first_name,
book.author.last_name)
```

In the above, we showed how to build relational models with foreign keys and many-to-many fields that connect our data entities in a meaningful way. Because of these connections, we can execute sophisticated queries and data manipulations.

Custom Model Methods

Overview

Standard Django models define the structure of your data with fields like CharField, IntegerField, DateField, and relationships like ForeignKey and ManyToManyField. These fields determine how data is stored in the database. However, models can also include custom methods that encapsulate business logic, making it easier to manage and manipulate data directly within the model.

Custom model methods differ from standard model fields in that they are not tied to the database schema. Instead, they provide additional functionality and behavior that operates on the data defined by the model. These methods can perform calculations, format data, or return subsets of data, allowing you to keep your logic organized and reusable.

Adding Custom Methods to Existing Model

We will enhance our existing Book and Author models in the BookTech application by adding some custom methods.

Adding a Custom Method to the Book Model

We will add a method to calculate the age of a book based on its publication date. Open library/models.py and modify the Book model to include the custom method:

```
from django.db import models

from datetime import date


class Author(models.Model):

    first_name = models.CharField(max_length=50)

    last_name = models.CharField(max_length=50)

    birth_date = models.DateField()


    def __str__(self):

        return f"{self.first_name} {self.last_name}"
```

```
class Publisher(models.Model):
    name = models.CharField(max_length=100)
    address = models.CharField(max_length=255)
    city = models.CharField(max_length=100)
    state_province = models.CharField(max_length=100)
    country = models.CharField(max_length=100)
    website = models.URLField()

    def __str__(self):
        return self.name

class Book(models.Model):
    title = models.CharField(max_length=200)
    author = models.ForeignKey(Author,
on_delete=models.CASCADE)
    publication_date = models.DateField()
    isbn = models.CharField(max_length=17)
    publishers = models.ManyToManyField(Publisher)

    def __str__(self):
        return self.title
```

```python
    def book_age(self):
        """Returns the age of the book in years."""
        today = date.today()
        return today.year - self.publication_date.year
```

The book_age method calculates the difference between the current year and the publication year of the book, returning the age of the book in years.

Adding a Custom Method to the Author Model

We will add a method to get the full name of an author.

```python
class Author(models.Model):
    first_name = models.CharField(max_length=50)
    last_name = models.CharField(max_length=50)
    birth_date = models.DateField()

    def __str__(self):
        return f"{self.first_name} {self.last_name}"

    def full_name(self):
        """Returns the full name of the author."""
        return f"{self.first_name} {self.last_name}"
```

The full_name method concatenates the first_name and last_name fields to return the full name of the author.

Adding a Custom Method to the Publisher Model

We will add a method to the Publisher model to format the publisher's address as a single string.

```
class Publisher(models.Model):

    name = models.CharField(max_length=100)

    address = models.CharField(max_length=255)

    city = models.CharField(max_length=100)

    state_province = models.CharField(max_length=100)

    country = models.CharField(max_length=100)

    website = models.URLField()


    def __str__(self):

        return self.name


    def formatted_address(self):

        """Returns the full address of the publisher."""

        return f"{self.address}, {self.city},
{self.state_province}, {self.country}"
```

The formatted_address method combines the address, city, state_province, and country fields into a single formatted string.

Using Custom Methods

Now that we have added custom methods to our models, we will use them in the Django shell.

- Enter the Django Shell:

```
python manage.py shell
```

- Create Instances:

```
from library.models import Author, Book, Publisher

from datetime import date


# Create authors

author1 = Author(first_name="John", last_name="Doe", birth_date="1970-01-01")

author1.save()

author2 = Author(first_name="Jane", last_name="Smith", birth_date="1980-05-15")

author2.save()


# Create publishers

publisher1 = Publisher(name="Tech Books Publishing", address="123 Main St", city="New York", state_province="NY", country="USA", website="http://techbooks.com")

publisher1.save()

publisher2 = Publisher(name="Knowledge Hub Publishing", address="456 Elm St", city="San Francisco", state_province="CA", country="USA", website="http://knowledgehub.com")

publisher2.save()
```

```
# Create books

book1 = Book(title="Learning Django", author=author1,
publication_date=date(2020, 1, 1), isbn="9781234567890")

book1.save()

book1.publishers.add(publisher1, publisher2)


book2 = Book(title="Advanced Django", author=author2,
publication_date=date(2018, 6, 1), isbn="9781234567891")

book2.save()

book2.publishers.add(publisher1)
```

- Use Custom Methods:

```
# Get the full name of the first author

print(author1.full_name())  # Output: John Doe


# Get the age of the first book

print(book1.book_age())  # Output: (current year - 2020)


# Get the formatted address of the first publisher

print(publisher1.formatted_address())  # Output: 123 Main
St, New York, NY, USA
```

Adding a Custom Method to Retrieve Related Data

We will add a method to the Author model to retrieve all books written by the author.

```
class Author(models.Model):

    first_name = models.CharField(max_length=50)

    last_name = models.CharField(max_length=50)

    birth_date = models.DateField()


    def __str__(self):

        return f"{self.first_name} {self.last_name}"


    def full_name(self):

        """Returns the full name of the author."""

        return f"{self.first_name} {self.last_name}"


    def get_books(self):

        """Returns all books written by the author."""

        return Book.objects.filter(author=self)
```

- Use the get_books Method:

```
# Get all books written by author1

books_by_author1 = author1.get_books()

for book in books_by_author1:

    print(book.title)  # Output: Learning Django
```

The above technique simplifies development by keeping code organized, readable, and reusable; it also makes managing complex business logic easier; and you can execute a variety of operations directly within your models.

Hands-on Lab: Create and query a book catalog

In this hands-on practical exercise, we will put together everything we've learned so far to create and query a book catalog for our BookTech application. This will involve defining models, applying migrations, creating instances, and querying the database using Django's ORM.

Define Models

We already have our Author, Book, and Publisher models defined. Given below is a recap of these models in library/models.py:

```
from django.db import models

from datetime import date



class Author(models.Model):

    first_name = models.CharField(max_length=50)

    last_name = models.CharField(max_length=50)

    birth_date = models.DateField()



    def __str__(self):

        return f"{self.first_name} {self.last_name}"



    def full_name(self):

        return f"{self.first_name} {self.last_name}"
```

```
    def get_books(self):
        return Book.objects.filter(author=self)


class Publisher(models.Model):
    name = models.CharField(max_length=100)
    address = models.CharField(max_length=255)
    city = models.CharField(max_length=100)
    state_province = models.CharField(max_length=100)
    country = models.CharField(max_length=100)
    website = models.URLField()


    def __str__(self):
        return self.name


    def formatted_address(self):
        return f"{self.address}, {self.city},
{self.state_province}, {self.country}"


class Book(models.Model):
    title = models.CharField(max_length=200)
    author = models.ForeignKey(Author,
on_delete=models.CASCADE)
```

```
    publication_date = models.DateField()
    isbn = models.CharField(max_length=17)
    publishers = models.ManyToManyField(Publisher)

    def __str__(self):
        return self.title

    def book_age(self):
        today = date.today()
        return today.year - self.publication_date.year
```

Apply Migrations

Ensure that your database schema is up to date by generating and applying the necessary migrations.

- Generate Migrations:

```
python manage.py makemigrations library
```

- Apply Migrations:

```
python manage.py migrate
```

Populate Database with Sample Data

Use the Django shell to create instances of Author, Publisher, and Book and establish relationships between them.

- Enter the Django Shell:

```
python manage.py shell
```

- Create Author Instances:

```
from library.models import Author, Book, Publisher

author1 = Author(first_name="John", last_name="Doe",
birth_date="1970-01-01")

author1.save()

author2 = Author(first_name="Jane", last_name="Smith",
birth_date="1980-05-15")

author2.save()
```

- Create Publisher Instances:

```
publisher1 = Publisher(name="Tech Books Publishing",
address="123 Main St", city="New York",
state_province="NY", country="USA",
website="http://techbooks.com")

publisher1.save()

publisher2 = Publisher(name="Knowledge Hub Publishing",
address="456 Elm St", city="San Francisco",
state_province="CA", country="USA",
website="http://knowledgehub.com")

publisher2.save()
```

- Create Book Instances and Associate with Authors and Publishers:

```
book1 = Book(title="Learning Django", author=author1,
publication_date="2020-01-01", isbn="9781234567890")

book1.save()

book1.publishers.add(publisher1, publisher2)
```

```
book2 = Book(title="Advanced Django", author=author2,
publication_date="2018-06-01", isbn="9781234567891")

book2.save()

book2.publishers.add(publisher1)
```

Query the Book Catalog

Now that we have populated the database with sample data, we will perform some queries to retrieve and display information.

- Retrieve All Books:

```
books = Book.objects.all()

for book in books:

    print(f"Title: {book.title}, Author:
{book.author.full_name()}, Publication Date:
{book.publication_date}, ISBN: {book.isbn}")
```

- Retrieve Books by a Specific Author:

```
books_by_author1 = Book.objects.filter(author=author1)

for book in books_by_author1:

    print(f"Title: {book.title}, Publication Date:
{book.publication_date}")
```

- Retrieve Books Published by a Specific Publisher:

```
books_by_publisher1 = publisher1.book_set.all()

for book in books_by_publisher1:
```

```
    print(f"Title: {book.title}, Author:
{book.author.full_name()}")
```

- Retrieve Books Published After a Certain Date:

```
books_published_after_2019 =
Book.objects.filter(publication_date__gt="2019-01-01")

for book in books_published_after_2019:

    print(f"Title: {book.title}, Publication Date:
{book.publication_date}")
```

Use Custom Methods in Queries:

```
# Get the age of each book

for book in books:

    print(f"Title: {book.title}, Age: {book.book_age()}
years")


# Get the full address of each publisher

for publisher in Publisher.objects.all():

    print(f"Publisher: {publisher.name}, Address:
{publisher.formatted_address()}")
```

Desired Output

We will see the output of our queries:

```
# Retrieve All Books

books = Book.objects.all()
```

```
for book in books:
    print(f"Title: {book.title}, Author:
{book.author.full_name()}, Publication Date:
{book.publication_date}, ISBN: {book.isbn}")

# Expected Output:
# Title: Learning Django, Author: John Doe, Publication
Date: 2020-01-01, ISBN: 9781234567890
# Title: Advanced Django, Author: Jane Smith, Publication
Date: 2018-06-01, ISBN: 9781234567891

# Retrieve Books by a Specific Author
books_by_author1 = Book.objects.filter(author=author1)
for book in books_by_author1:
    print(f"Title: {book.title}, Publication Date:
{book.publication_date}")

# Expected Output:
# Title: Learning Django, Publication Date: 2020-01-01

# Retrieve Books Published by a Specific Publisher
books_by_publisher1 = publisher1.book_set.all()
for book in books_by_publisher1:
```

```
    print(f"Title: {book.title}, Author:
{book.author.full_name()}")


# Expected Output:

# Title: Learning Django, Author: John Doe

# Title: Advanced Django, Author: Jane Smith


# Retrieve Books Published After a Certain Date

books_published_after_2019 =
Book.objects.filter(publication_date__gt="2019-01-01")

for book in books_published_after_2019:

    print(f"Title: {book.title}, Publication Date:
{book.publication_date}")


# Expected Output:

# Title: Learning Django, Publication Date: 2020-01-01


# Use Custom Methods in Queries

for book in books:

    print(f"Title: {book.title}, Age: {book.book_age()}
years")


for publisher in Publisher.objects.all():
```

```
    print(f"Publisher: {publisher.name}, Address:
{publisher.formatted_address()}")


# Expected Output:

# Title: Learning Django, Age: 3 years (assuming current
year is 2023)

# Title: Advanced Django, Age: 5 years (assuming current
year is 2023)

# Publisher: Tech Books Publishing, Address: 123 Main St,
New York, NY, USA

# Publisher: Knowledge Hub Publishing, Address: 456 Elm
St, San Francisco, CA, USA
```

Using what we've learned about Django models, relationships, migrations, and custom methods, we built and queried a book catalog for the BookTech app in the above practical lab. This exercise showed how to use Django's object-relational mapping (ORM) to define models, manage the database schema, insert sample data into the database, and run queries.

Summary

In this chapter, we looked at Django models and the ORM framework, which allows developers to interact with databases through Python code rather than SQL. We then defined the Book, Author, and Publisher models for the BookTech application, building associations between them via foreign keys and many-to-many fields.

We next moved on to database migrations, where we learnt how to maintain the database structure aligned with the models. We practiced creating and implementing migrations to ensure that the database mirrored the current state of our application. We created custom model methods to improve the usefulness of our models. These methods enclosed business logic, making tasks easy to complete directly within the model. Examples include determining a book's age, returning an author's full name, and formatting a publisher's address, which adds functionality to the basic model fields.

We also experimented with the ORM, learning how to do CRUD operations and complicated queries. We used the Django shell to create, retrieve, update, and delete records, illustrating the ORM's strength and versatility. Queries include filtering books by author, retrieving books released by a specified publisher, and retrieving related data through bespoke methods. Working with models and the ORM in such an overall manner helped us better understand how to handle and interact with data in a Django project, which in turn made development more intuitive and efficient.

Test Your Knowledge

1. What is a Django model?

a) A Python class that defines the structure and behavior of a web page
b) A template file that contains HTML for rendering web pages
c) A Python class that represents a database table
d) A JavaScript function for handling client-side interactions

Answer: c) A Python class that represents a database table

2. Which command is used to generate migration files after modifying a model?

a) python manage.py migrate
b) python manage.py create_migration
c) python manage.py makemigrations
d) python manage.py update_migration

Answer: c) python manage.py makemigrations

3. How do you apply migrations to update the database schema?

a) python manage.py applymigrations
b) python manage.py migrate
c) python manage.py syncdb
d) python manage.py updatedb

Answer: b) python manage.py migrate

4. What is the purpose of a ForeignKey in Django models?

a) To create a one-to-one relationship between models
b) To create a one-to-many relationship between models
c) To create a many-to-many relationship between models
d) To define the primary key of a model

Answer: b) To create a one-to-many relationship between models

5. Which field type would you use to establish a many-to-many relationship in Django models?

a) ForeignKey

b) OneToOneField
c) ManyToManyField
d) PrimaryKeyField

Answer: c) ManyToManyField

6. What does the on_delete=models.CASCADE argument specify in a ForeignKey field?

a) That the related field should be nullified when the referenced object is deleted
b) That the related field should be set to a default value when the referenced object is deleted
c) That the related field should raise an error when the referenced object is deleted
d) That the related objects should also be deleted when the referenced object is deleted

Answer: d) That the related objects should also be deleted when the referenced object is deleted

7. What Django ORM method would you use to retrieve all books written by a specific author?

a) Book.filter(author=author)
b) Book.get(author=author)
c) Book.objects.filter(author=author)
d) Book.objects.get(author=author)

Answer: c) Book.objects.filter(author=author)

8. Which command is used to open the Django shell for interactive work with models and data?

a) python manage.py openshell
b) python manage.py shell
c) python manage.py start
d) python manage.py console

Answer: b) python manage.py shell

CHAPTER 3: VIEWS AND URL ROUTING

Introduction

The purpose of this chapter is to find out how Django manages web requests and maps them to the specific views that are required. We will begin with gaining a knowledge of the idea of views in Django, specifically comparing and contrasting function-based views (FBVs) and class-based views (CBVs). The next topic that we will cover is URL routing, which will teach you how to map URLs to views by utilizing the URL configuration system that Django provides. Among these will be the configuration of static and dynamic routes, which will make it possible for you to generate URLs that are able to adjust to different types of content and user inputs.

After that, we will learn the processing of forms in views, during which you will learn how to process and validate form data within your views respectively. In addition, we will explore view decorators, which offer a method to improve and modify the behavior of your views without affecting the fundamental logic of such views.

To reinforce your learning, the chapter concludes with an interactive exercise in which you will create a book detail and list view for the BookTech application. You will gain practical experience in building and managing views and URL routing in a Django application by participating in this hands-on exercise, which will bring together all of the ideas that were learned in the chapter.

Understanding Views

Introduction to Views in Django

A view is a Python function or class that receives a web request and returns a web response. It acts as a bridge between the user and the data, processing the user's request, interacting with the model, and returning the appropriate response, often rendered as HTML. Views encapsulate the logic necessary to render a page and determine what data to display.

When a request is made to a Django application, the URL routing mechanism maps the URL to a specific view. This view then processes the request, performs any required operations (such as querying the database), and returns a response. This response can be an HTML page, a redirect, a JSON object, or any other type of web content.

Function-Based Views (FBVs)

Function-based views are simple Python functions that take a web request and return a web response. They are straightforward to understand and use, making them a good starting point for beginners. Given below is an example of a function-based view:

```
from django.http import HttpResponse

from django.shortcuts import render
```

```
from .models import Book


def book_list(request):
    books = Book.objects.all()
    return render(request, 'library/book_list.html',
{'books': books})
```

In the above given code snippet, the book_list function receives an HTTP request, queries the Book model to retrieve all book instances, and renders the book_list.html template with the list of books.

Class-Based Views (CBVs)

Class-based views offer more structure and reusability by using Python classes to define views. They can encapsulate multiple methods to handle different HTTP methods (GET, POST, etc.) within a single class, providing a cleaner and more organized way to manage views. Following is an example of a class-based view:

```
from django.views.generic import ListView
from .models import Book


class BookListView(ListView):
    model = Book
    template_name = 'library/book_list.html'
    context_object_name = 'books'
```

In the above given code snippet, BookListView inherits from Django's ListView, which is a built-in generic view for displaying a list of objects. The class specifies the model to query, the template to render, and the context object name for the template.

Applicability of Function-Based and Class-Based Views

Both function-based views and class-based views have their own advantages and are suitable for different scenarios.

- Function-Based Views:
    - FBVs are simple and straightforward, making them ideal for small projects or simple views where the overhead of creating a class is unnecessary.
    - Since FBVs are just functions, the flow of the code is explicit and easy to follow.
- Class-Based Views:
    - CBVs promote code reuse by allowing you to inherit from generic views and other custom views. This reduces the need to write repetitive code.
    - CBVs provide a more organized structure, especially for complex views with multiple actions and methods.
    - CBVs can be easily extended and customized, making them suitable for large applications with complex requirements.

Sample Program: Function-based View for List of Books

We will create a function-based view for displaying a list of books and another for displaying details of a specific book.

Book List View

```
from django.http import HttpResponse

from django.shortcuts import render

from .models import Book


def book_list(request):

    books = Book.objects.all()

    return render(request, 'library/book_list.html',
{'books': books})
```

Book Detail View

```
from django.http import HttpResponse

from django.shortcuts import render, get_object_or_404

from .models import Book


def book_detail(request, book_id):

    book = get_object_or_404(Book, id=book_id)

    return render(request, 'library/book_detail.html',
{'book': book})
```

Sample Program: Class-based View for List of Books

We will create equivalent class-based views for the same functionality.

Book List View

```
from django.views.generic import ListView

from .models import Book


class BookListView(ListView):

    model = Book

    template_name = 'library/book_list.html'

    context_object_name = 'books'
```

Book Detail View

```
from django.views.generic import DetailView

from .models import Book
```

```
class BookDetailView(DetailView):
    model = Book
    template_name = 'library/book_detail.html'
    context_object_name = 'book'
```

Choosing the best view type for your needs is something you'll get better at as you progress through the chapter. With the information in this chapter, you should be able to construct a strong and organized BookTech application that makes use of both kinds.

Mapping URLs to Views

Overview

URL configuration in Django involves mapping URL patterns to views. This mapping is defined in the urls.py file, which acts as a table of contents for your application, directing incoming requests to the appropriate view functions or classes. By setting up URL configurations, you ensure that users can access different parts of your application through well-defined routes.

Setting up URL Configurations

To demonstrate how to set up URL configurations, we will use the BookTech application and map URLs to both function-based and class-based views we learned earlier.

Project-level URL Configuration

First, ensure your project's main urls.py file includes the URL patterns for the library app. Open BookTech/urls.py and update it as follows:

```
from django.contrib import admin
from django.urls import path, include


urlpatterns = [
```

```
    path('admin/', admin.site.urls),
    path('library/', include('library.urls')),
]
```

This configuration includes the library app's URL patterns under the library/ path.

App-level URL Configuration

Next, create a urls.py file in the library app directory if it doesn't already exist. This file will contain the URL patterns specific to the library app.

```
touch library/urls.py
```

Define URL Patterns for Function-Based Views

Open library/urls.py and define URL patterns for the function-based views:

```
from django.urls import path
from . import views


urlpatterns = [
    path('books/', views.book_list, name='book_list'),
    path('books/<int:book_id>/', views.book_detail,
name='book_detail'),
]
```

In this configuration:

- path('books/', views.book_list, name='book_list') maps the books/ URL to the book_list view.
- path('books/<int:book_id>/', views.book_detail, name='book_detail') maps URLs like books/1/ to the book_detail view, capturing the book_id as an integer parameter.

Define URL Patterns for Class-Based Views

To map URLs to class-based views, we use the as_view() method. Update library/urls.py to include the class-based views:

```
from django.urls import path

from .views import BookListView, BookDetailView


urlpatterns = [

    path('books/', BookListView.as_view(),
name='book_list'),

    path('books/<int:pk>/', BookDetailView.as_view(),
name='book_detail'),

]
```

In this configuration:

- path('books/', BookListView.as_view(), name='book_list') maps the books/ URL to the BookListView class-based view.
- path('books/<int:pk>/', BookDetailView.as_view(), name='book_detail') maps URLs like books/1/ to the BookDetailView class-based view, using pk (primary key) as the parameter.

Combining Function-Based and Class-Based Views

You can mix function-based and class-based views in the same urls.py file. Following is an example that includes both:

```
from django.urls import path

from . import views

from .views import BookListView, BookDetailView
```

```
urlpatterns = [

    # Function-Based Views

    path('fbv/books/', views.book_list,
name='book_list_fbv'),

    path('fbv/books/<int:book_id>/', views.book_detail,
name='book_detail_fbv'),


    # Class-Based Views

    path('cbv/books/', BookListView.as_view(),
name='book_list_cbv'),

    path('cbv/books/<int:pk>/', BookDetailView.as_view(),
name='book_detail_cbv'),

]
```

In this configuration:

- path('fbv/books/', views.book_list, name='book_list_fbv') maps to the function-based book_list view.
- path('fbv/books/<int:book_id>/', views.book_detail, name='book_detail_fbv') maps to the function-based book_detail view.
- path('cbv/books/', BookListView.as_view(), name='book_list_cbv') maps to the class-based BookListView.
- path('cbv/books/<int:pk>/', BookDetailView.as_view(), name='book_detail_cbv') maps to the class-based BookDetailView.

Testing the URL Configurations

To verify that the URL configurations are working correctly, start the Django development server:

```
python manage.py runserver
```

Open your web browser and navigate to the following URLs:

- http://127.0.0.1:8000/library/fbv/books/ should display the list of books using the function-based view.
- http://127.0.0.1:8000/library/fbv/books/1/ should display the details of the book with ID 1 using the function-based view.
- http://127.0.0.1:8000/library/cbv/books/ should display the list of books using the class-based view.
- http://127.0.0.1:8000/library/cbv/books/1/ should display the details of the book with ID 1 using the class-based view.

You can make your application easy to extend and maintain by organizing it logically using the structure mentioned above. Users can access different views through well-defined URLs with the above configurations.

Dynamic Routing

Concept of Dynamic Routing

Dynamic routing in Django involves creating URLs that can accept variable data, making your web application more interactive and flexible. Instead of hardcoding URLs, dynamic routes allow you to capture parts of the URL as parameters, which can be passed to views to retrieve or process data. This is particularly useful for applications where you need to display details of specific items, handle user profiles, or filter content based on certain criteria.

For example, in an e-commerce application, dynamic routing enables URLs like /products/42/ to show details for the product with ID 42. Similarly, in the BookTech application, you can use dynamic routing to display details of specific books or filter books by author or genre.

Sample Program: Creating URLs with Dynamic Content

To demonstrate dynamic routing, we will create URLs in the BookTech application that capture book IDs and display corresponding book details.

Setting up Models

Ensure your models are set up in library/models.py:

```
from django.db import models


class Author(models.Model):
```

```
    first_name = models.CharField(max_length=50)

    last_name = models.CharField(max_length=50)

    birth_date = models.DateField()


    def __str__(self):

        return f"{self.first_name} {self.last_name}"


class Publisher(models.Model):

    name = models.CharField(max_length=100)

    address = models.CharField(max_length=255)

    city = models.CharField(max_length=100)

    state_province = models.CharField(max_length=100)

    country = models.CharField(max_length=100)

    website = models.URLField()


    def __str__(self):

        return self.name


class Book(models.Model):

    title = models.CharField(max_length=200)

    author = models.ForeignKey(Author,
on_delete=models.CASCADE)
```

```
    publication_date = models.DateField()
    isbn = models.CharField(max_length=17)
    publishers = models.ManyToManyField(Publisher)

    def __str__(self):
        return self.title
```

Creating Views with Dynamic Routing

Update or create views in library/views.py to handle dynamic routing. We will create a view to display details of a specific book based on its ID.

```
from django.shortcuts import render, get_object_or_404
from .models import Book


def book_detail(request, book_id):
    book = get_object_or_404(Book, id=book_id)
    return render(request, 'library/book_detail.html',
{'book': book})
```

Defining URL Patterns with Dynamic Segments

Update library/urls.py to include a dynamic URL pattern that captures the book ID from the URL and passes it to the book_detail view.

```
from django.urls import path
from . import views
```

```
urlpatterns = [

    path('books/', views.book_list, name='book_list'),

    path('books/<int:book_id>/', views.book_detail,
name='book_detail'),

]
```

In this configuration, the <int:book_id>/ part of the URL pattern captures an integer from the URL and passes it as the book_id parameter to the book_detail view.

Creating Templates for Dynamic Content

Create a template to display the book details. Create library/templates/library/book_detail.html with the following content:

```
<!DOCTYPE html>

<html>

<head>

    <title>{{ book.title }}</title>

</head>

<body>

    <h1>{{ book.title }}</h1>

    <p><strong>Author:</strong> {{ book.author.first_name
}} {{ book.author.last_name }}</p>

    <p><strong>Publication Date:</strong> {{
book.publication_date }}</p>

    <p><strong>ISBN:</strong> {{ book.isbn }}</p>

    <p><strong>Publishers:</strong>
```

```
        <ul>
            {% for publisher in book.publishers.all %}
                <li>{{ publisher.name }}</li>
            {% endfor %}
        </ul>
    </p>
</body>
</html>
```

Testing Dynamic Routing

To test the dynamic routing setup, start the Django development server and navigate to a URL that includes a book ID, such as http://127.0.0.1:8000/library/books/1/. If a book with ID 1 exists, you should see the book details displayed using the book_detail.html template.

Creating View to List Books with Links to Dynamic Routes

To fully utilize dynamic routing, we can create a view that lists all books with links to their detail pages. Update library/views.py to include a book list view:

```
def book_list(request):
    books = Book.objects.all()
    return render(request, 'library/book_list.html',
{'books': books})
```

Create the corresponding template library/templates/library/book_list.html:

```
<!DOCTYPE html>
<html>
```

```
<head>
    <title>Book List</title>
</head>
<body>
    <h1>Book List</h1>
    <ul>
        {% for book in books %}
                <li><a href="{% url 'book_detail' book.id
%}">{{ book.title }}</a></li>
        {% endfor %}
    </ul>
</body>
</html>
```

In this template, {% url 'book_detail' book.id %} generates the URL for the book_detail view with the appropriate book ID.

Expanding Dynamic Routing with Complex URLs

Dynamic routing can be extended to capture multiple parameters or handle more complex URL structures. For example, if we want to filter books by author, we can add a new view and URL pattern:

- Add View for Books by Author:

```
def books_by_author(request, author_id):
    author = get_object_or_404(Author, id=author_id)
    books = Book.objects.filter(author=author)
```

```
    return render(request,
'library/books_by_author.html', {'author': author,
'books': books})
```

- Update URL Patterns:

```
urlpatterns = [

    path('books/', views.book_list, name='book_list'),

    path('books/<int:book_id>/', views.book_detail,
name='book_detail'),

    path('authors/<int:author_id>/books/',
views.books_by_author, name='books_by_author'),

]
```

- Create Template for Books by Author:

```
<!DOCTYPE html>

<html>

<head>

    <title>Books by {{ author.first_name }} {{
author.last_name }}</title>

</head>

<body>

    <h1>Books by {{ author.first_name }} {{
author.last_name }}</h1>

    <ul>

        {% for book in books %}
```

```
            <li><a href="{% url 'book_detail' book.id
%}">{{ book.title }}</a></li>

        {% endfor %}

    </ul>

</body>

</html>
```

This setup allows users to view all books by a specific author using a URL like http://127.0.0.1:8000/library/authors/1/books/.

As we saw above, dynamic routing allows you to generate URLs that are responsive to the inputs and data provided by users, thereby enhancing the level of interactivity and user-friendliness of your web application.

Handling Forms in Views

Overview

Forms are a crucial part of web applications, allowing users to submit data, which can then be processed and stored. The forms can be handled using the forms module, which provides tools for generating HTML forms, validating submitted data, and processing it in views. By using Django forms, you can ensure that the data entered by users is clean and conforms to the expected format before it is processed or saved.

Setting up a Form

To demonstrate handling forms in views, we will create a form for adding new books to the BookTech application.

Creating a Form Class

First, create a form class for the Book model. In your library app, create a file named forms.py:

```
touch library/forms.py
```

Then, define the form class in library/forms.py:

```
from django import forms
from .models import Book


class BookForm(forms.ModelForm):
    class Meta:
        model = Book
        fields = ['title', 'author', 'publication_date',
'isbn', 'publishers']
```

The BookForm class uses forms.ModelForm to create a form that maps to the Book model, including fields for the book's title, author, publication date, ISBN, and publishers.

Creating the View to Handle the Form

Next, create a view to handle displaying the form and processing the submitted data. Open library/views.py and add the following view:

```
from django.shortcuts import render, redirect
from .forms import BookForm


def add_book(request):
    if request.method == 'POST':
        form = BookForm(request.POST)
        if form.is_valid():
            form.save()
            return redirect('book_list')
```

```
    else:

        form = BookForm()

    return render(request, 'library/add_book.html',
{'form': form})
```

In this view:

- If the request method is POST, it means the form has been submitted. The view then creates a BookForm instance with the submitted data and checks if it is valid.
- If the form is valid, the data is saved to the database, and the user is redirected to the book list view.
- If the request method is not POST, an empty form is created and displayed.

Defining URL Pattern for the View

Update library/urls.py to include a URL pattern for the add_book view:

```
from django.urls import path

from . import views



urlpatterns = [

    path('books/', views.book_list, name='book_list'),

    path('books/<int:book_id>/', views.book_detail,
name='book_detail'),

    path('books/add/', views.add_book, name='add_book'),

]
```

Creating the Template for the Form

Create a template to display the form.

Create a file named library/templates/library/add_book.html with the following content:

```
<!DOCTYPE html>
<html>
<head>
    <title>Add Book</title>
</head>
<body>
    <h1>Add a New Book</h1>
    <form method="post">
        {% csrf_token %}
        {{ form.as_p }}
        <button type="submit">Save</button>
    </form>
</body>
</html>
```

In this template:

- {% csrf_token %} is a security feature to prevent Cross-Site Request Forgery (CSRF) attacks.
- {{ form.as_p }} renders the form fields as HTML paragraphs.

After you launch the server, navigate to http://127.0.0.1:8000/library/books/add/. You should see the form to add a new book. Fill in the form and submit it to test if the book is added to the database and if you are redirected to the book list view.

Validating Form Data

Django forms automatically handle basic validation, such as ensuring required fields are filled out and data types are correct. You can add custom validation by overriding the clean method in your form class. For example, if you want to ensure that the ISBN is exactly 13 characters long, you can add this validation:

```
class BookForm(forms.ModelForm):

    class Meta:

        model = Book

        fields = ['title', 'author', 'publication_date',
'isbn', 'publishers']


    def clean_isbn(self):

        isbn = self.cleaned_data.get('isbn')

        if len(isbn) != 13:

            raise forms.ValidationError("ISBN must be
exactly 13 characters long.")

        return isbn
```

With this custom validation, if the submitted ISBN is not 13 characters long, the form will not be valid, and an error message will be displayed.

Handling Multiple Form Types in a Single View

Sometimes, you might need to handle multiple forms in a single view. For instance, if you want to allow adding a new author along with the book, you can handle both forms in the same view. Following is an example of how to do that:

- Add Author Form:

```
from .models import Author


class AuthorForm(forms.ModelForm):

    class Meta:
```

```
        model = Author
        fields = ['first_name', 'last_name', 'birth_date']
```

- Update the View:

```
from .forms import BookForm, AuthorForm


def add_book_and_author(request):
    if request.method == 'POST':
        book_form = BookForm(request.POST)
        author_form = AuthorForm(request.POST)
        if book_form.is_valid() and author_form.is_valid():
            author = author_form.save()
            book = book_form.save(commit=False)
            book.author = author
            book.save()
            return redirect('book_list')
    else:
        book_form = BookForm()
        author_form = AuthorForm()
```

```
    return render(request,
'library/add_book_and_author.html', {'book_form':
book_form, 'author_form': author_form})
```

- Update URL Patterns:

```
urlpatterns = [
    path('books/', views.book_list, name='book_list'),
    path('books/<int:book_id>/', views.book_detail,
name='book_detail'),
    path('books/add/', views.add_book, name='add_book'),
    path('books/add_with_author/',
views.add_book_and_author, name='add_book_and_author'),
]
```

- Create the Template:

```
<!DOCTYPE html>
<html>
<head>
    <title>Add Book and Author</title>
</head>
<body>
    <h1>Add a New Book and Author</h1>
    <form method="post">
        {% csrf_token %}
```

```
        <h2>Book Information</h2>

        {{ book_form.as_p }}

        <h2>Author Information</h2>

        {{ author_form.as_p }}

        <button type="submit">Save</button>

    </form>

</body>

</html>
```

With this setup, you can add both a new book and a new author in a single form submission. The view processes both forms, validates the data, and saves the objects to the database.

View Decorators

Overview

In Python, decorators are a powerful and flexible tool that allow you to modify the behavior of a function or class. Decorators are functions that wrap another function or method, adding some functionality before or after the wrapped function is called. The decorators are commonly used to enhance views with additional features such as access control, caching, and request handling.

Understanding Django View Decorators

Django provides several built-in decorators to enhance the functionality of your views. Some of the most commonly used decorators include:

- @login_required: Ensures that the user is authenticated before accessing the view.
- @permission_required: Checks if the user has a specific permission before accessing the view.
- @csrf_exempt: Exempts the view from CSRF protection.
- @require_http_methods: Restricts the view to specific HTTP methods (e.g., GET, POST).

Using a Single Decorator

We will enhance the add_book view from our previous examples by ensuring that only authenticated users can add new books. We will use the @login_required decorator.

Update View with a Decorator

Open library/views.py and import the login_required decorator. Then, apply it to the add_book view:

```
from django.contrib.auth.decorators import login_required

from django.shortcuts import render, redirect

from .forms import BookForm



@login_required

def add_book(request):

    if request.method == 'POST':

        form = BookForm(request.POST)

        if form.is_valid():

            form.save()

            return redirect('book_list')

    else:

        form = BookForm()

    return render(request, 'library/add_book.html',
{'form': form})
```

The @login_required decorator ensures that only authenticated users can access the add_book view. If an unauthenticated user tries to access this view, they will be redirected to the login page.

After you launch the server, navigate to http://127.0.0.1:8000/library/books/add/. If you are not logged in, you will be redirected to the login page.

Using Multiple Decorators

You can stack multiple decorators on a single view to combine their functionalities. For example, we will enhance the add_book view further by requiring that the user has a specific permission to add books.

Update View with Multiple Decorators

Open library/views.py and import the permission_required decorator. Then, apply both the login_required and permission_required decorators to the add_book view:

```
from django.contrib.auth.decorators import
login_required, permission_required

from django.shortcuts import render, redirect

from .forms import BookForm



@login_required

@permission_required('library.add_book',
raise_exception=True)

def add_book(request):

    if request.method == 'POST':

        form = BookForm(request.POST)

        if form.is_valid():

            form.save()

            return redirect('book_list')

    else:

        form = BookForm()
```

```
    return render(request, 'library/add_book.html',
{'form': form})
```

The @permission_required decorator checks if the user has the library.add_book permission. If the user does not have this permission, a PermissionDenied exception is raised.

After you launch the server, navigate to http://127.0.0.1:8000/library/books/add/. If you are logged in but do not have the library.add_book permission, you will see a permission denied error. If you have the required permission, you can access the view and add a new book.

Creating Custom Decorators

In addition to using built-in decorators, you can create your own custom decorators to add specific functionality to your views. We will create a custom decorator that logs the time taken to execute a view.

Creating a Custom Decorator

Create a file named library/decorators.py and define the custom decorator:

```
import time

from functools import wraps

from django.http import HttpResponse


def log_execution_time(view_func):

    @wraps(view_func)

    def _wrapped_view(request, *args, **kwargs):

        start_time = time.time()

        response = view_func(request, *args, **kwargs)

        end_time = time.time()

        execution_time = end_time - start_time
```

```
        print(f"Execution time for {view_func.__name__}:
{execution_time} seconds")

        return response

    return _wrapped_view
```

The log_execution_time decorator calculates the time taken to execute the wrapped view and prints it to the console.

Applying Custom Decorator to a View

Open library/views.py and import the custom decorator. Then, apply it to the add_book view:

```
from django.contrib.auth.decorators import
login_required, permission_required

from django.shortcuts import render, redirect

from .forms import BookForm

from .decorators import log_execution_time


@log_execution_time

@login_required

@permission_required('library.add_book',
raise_exception=True)

def add_book(request):

    if request.method == 'POST':

        form = BookForm(request.POST)

        if form.is_valid():

            form.save()
```

```
            return redirect('book_list')
    else:
        form = BookForm()
    return render(request, 'library/add_book.html',
{'form': form})
```

The log_execution_time decorator logs the execution time of the add_book view.

After you launch the server, navigate to http://127.0.0.1:8000/library/books/add/. After submitting the form, check the console to see the execution time logged by the custom decorator. Your code is made more modular and reusable by utilizing decorators to add extra functionality to your views.

Interactive Task

In this hands-on practical exercise, we will apply the concepts and skills learned so far to build a detailed view and a list view for books in our BookTech application. We will create views, templates, and URL configurations to display a list of all books and detailed information for each book.

Define the Models

Ensure that the Book, Author, and Publisher models are defined in library/models.py:

```
from django.db import models


class Author(models.Model):
    first_name = models.CharField(max_length=50)
    last_name = models.CharField(max_length=50)
    birth_date = models.DateField()
```

```
    def __str__(self):
        return f"{self.first_name} {self.last_name}"


class Publisher(models.Model):
    name = models.CharField(max_length=100)
    address = models.CharField(max_length=255)
    city = models.CharField(max_length=100)
    state_province = models.CharField(max_length=100)
    country = models.CharField(max_length=100)
    website = models.URLField()

    def __str__(self):
        return self.name


class Book(models.Model):
    title = models.CharField(max_length=200)
    author = models.ForeignKey(Author,
on_delete=models.CASCADE)
    publication_date = models.DateField()
    isbn = models.CharField(max_length=17)
    publishers = models.ManyToManyField(Publisher)
```

```
    def __str__(self):
        return self.title
```

Create Views for Book List and Book Detail

Book List View

Open library/views.py and create a function-based view to display the list of books:

```
from django.shortcuts import render
from .models import Book


def book_list(request):
    books = Book.objects.all()
    return render(request, 'library/book_list.html',
{'books': books})
```

Book Detail View

Create another function-based view to display the details of a specific book:

```
from django.shortcuts import render, get_object_or_404
from .models import Book


def book_detail(request, book_id):
    book = get_object_or_404(Book, id=book_id)
    return render(request, 'library/book_detail.html',
{'book': book})
```

Define URL Patterns

Update library/urls.py to include URL patterns for the book list and book detail views:

```
from django.urls import path

from . import views


urlpatterns = [

    path('books/', views.book_list, name='book_list'),

    path('books/<int:book_id>/', views.book_detail,
name='book_detail'),

]
```

Create Templates

Book List Template

Create a template to display the list of books. Create library/templates/library/book_list.html with the following content:

```
<!DOCTYPE html>

<html>

<head>

    <title>Book List</title>

</head>

<body>

    <h1>Book List</h1>

    <ul>
```

```
        {% for book in books %}

            <li><a href="{% url 'book_detail' book.id
%}">{{ book.title }}</a> by {{ book.author.first_name }}
{{ book.author.last_name }}</li>

        {% endfor %}

    </ul>

</body>

</html>
```

This template generates a list of links to the detail pages for each book.

Book Detail Template

- Create a template to display the details of a specific book.
- Create library/templates/library/book_detail.html with the following content:

```
<!DOCTYPE html>

<html>

<head>

    <title>{{ book.title }}</title>

</head>

<body>

    <h1>{{ book.title }}</h1>

    <p><strong>Author:</strong> {{ book.author.first_name
}} {{ book.author.last_name }}</p>

    <p><strong>Publication Date:</strong> {{
book.publication_date }}</p>
```

```
    <p><strong>ISBN:</strong> {{ book.isbn }}</p>

    <p><strong>Publishers:</strong>

        <ul>

            {% for publisher in book.publishers.all %}

                <li>{{ publisher.name }}</li>

            {% endfor %}

        </ul>

    </p>

    <p><a href="{% url 'book_list' %}">Back to book
list</a></p>

</body>

</html>
```

This template displays detailed information about the selected book.

After you launch the server, navigate to the following URLs to test the views:

- http://127.0.0.1:8000/library/books/ to see the list of books.
- http://127.0.0.1:8000/library/books/1/ to see the details of the book with ID 1.

Enhancing Views with Class-Based Views

If you prefer to use class-based views, you can convert the function-based views to class-based views.

Book List View

```
from django.views.generic import ListView

from .models import Book
```

```
class BookListView(ListView):
    model = Book
    template_name = 'library/book_list.html'
    context_object_name = 'books'
```

Book Detail View

```
from django.views.generic import DetailView
from .models import Book


class BookDetailView(DetailView):
    model = Book
    template_name = 'library/book_detail.html'
    context_object_name = 'book'
```

Update URL Patterns

Update library/urls.py to use the class-based views:

```
from django.urls import path
from .views import BookListView, BookDetailView


urlpatterns = [
    path('books/', BookListView.as_view(),
name='book_list'),
```

```
    path('books/<int:pk>/', BookDetailView.as_view(),
name='book_detail'),
]
```

The above instructions helped us build a class-based view and a function-based view for the BookTech app's book catalog and detail pages. This all-inclusive task shows how to construct a full feature in a Django app by integrating views, URL configurations, and templates.

Summary

All in all, we delved into Django's view system and URL routing. We started by learning the role of views in Django, which served as a link between the user and the data, processing requests and returning results. We studied the differences between function-based views (FBVs) and class-based views (CBVs), concluding that FBVs are simpler and more explicit, whereas CBVs provide higher reusability and structure for complicated systems.

We next moved on to URL routing, learning how to map URLs to views in Django using the URL configuration system. We configured URLs at the project and app levels, allowing users to access various portions of the application via well-defined routes. We also explored dynamic routing by establishing URLs that capture book IDs and display the related book data. We then worked on handling forms in views, creating a form for adding new books to the BookTech application. We established a form class, built a view to handle the form, configured URL patterns, and designed templates to render the form and display submitted data.

Finally, we learned view decorators, which change the behavior of views. We used built-in decorators to manage view access, such as @login_required and @permission_required. We also constructed a custom decorator to log the execution time of a view, followed by a hands-on program in which we used these concepts to build a book detail and list view, combining views, URL configurations, and templates into a comprehensive feature for the BookTech application.

Test Your Knowledge

1. What is the primary purpose of a view in Django?

a) To define the structure of the database
b) To render templates and manage URL patterns
c) To process web requests and return web responses
d) To manage static files and media

Answer: c) To process web requests and return web responses

2. Which decorator is used to ensure that a user is authenticated before accessing a view?

a) @permission_required
b) @csrf_exempt
c) @login_required
d) @require_http_methods

Answer: c) @login_required

3. How do you map a URL to a function-based view in Django?

a) By defining the URL pattern in the views.py file
b) By mapping the URL pattern in the settings.py file
c) By using the path() function in the urls.py file
d) By creating a URL route in the admin.py file

Answer: c) By using the path() function in the urls.py file

4. What is the main difference between function-based views (FBVs) and class-based views (CBVs)?

a) FBVs are used for smaller projects, while CBVs are used for larger projects
b) FBVs are simpler and more explicit, while CBVs offer greater reusability and organization
c) FBVs do not support decorators, while CBVs do
d) FBVs can only handle GET requests, while CBVs can handle all types of HTTP requests

Answer: b) FBVs are simpler and more explicit, while CBVs offer greater reusability and organization

5. Which method in a class-based view is used to handle GET requests?

a) get()
b) post()
c) dispatch()
d) as_view()

Answer: a) get()

6. What is dynamic routing in Django?

a) Creating static URL patterns
b) Creating URLs that can accept variable data
c) Defining URL patterns in the models.py file
d) Mapping URLs to static files

Answer: b) Creating URLs that can accept variable data

7. Which of the following URL patterns captures a book ID and passes it to the view?

a) path('books/', views.book_list, name='book_list')
b) path('books/<int:book_id>/', views.book_detail, name='book_detail')

c) path('books/<str:book_title>/', views.book_detail, name='book_detail')
d) path('books/detail/', views.book_detail, name='book_detail')

Answer: b) path('books/<int:book_id>/', views.book_detail, name='book_detail')

8. How do you process form data in a Django view?

a) By defining the form fields in the settings.py file
b) By creating a form class in forms.py and handling it in the view
c) By adding the form HTML directly into the view function
d) By using the csrf_exempt decorator

Answer: b) By creating a form class in forms.py and handling it in the view

9. Which decorator exempts a view from CSRF protection?

a) @login_required
b) @permission_required
c) @require_http_methods
d) @csrf_exempt

Answer: d) @csrf_exempt

10. How do you apply multiple decorators to a single view in Django?

a) By stacking them one after another above the view function
b) By placing them inside the view function
c) By defining them in the urls.py file
d) By using the as_view() method

Answer: a) By stacking them one after another above the view function

CHAPTER 4: TEMPLATES AND DJANGO'S TEMPLATE LANGUAGE

Introduction

The goal of this chapter is to develop dynamic and visually appealing web pages utilizing Django's sophisticated templating mechanism. We will begin by configuring Django templates and learning how to construct and use them to generate HTML text. This core understanding will allow you to properly create static and dynamic web pages. Then, we will look at template inheritance, which lets you create a base template and extend it using child templates. You'll learn how to create basic templates and override particular portions in child templates to tailor information to different sites.

We will also look at template tags and filters, which are useful for adding logic and formatting to your templates. You will learn about built-in tags and filters, as well as how to develop your own to fulfill special requirements. This allows you to conduct things like looping through data, conditionally displaying material, and formatting dates and numbers right within your designs. In addition, we will go over how to move data from views to templates using context, ensuring that your templates have access to the data they need to render.

Finally, we will go over several tools and strategies for debugging templates, which will help you detect and resolve errors more rapidly. At the end of the chapter, you'll be asked to put all that you've learned into practice by designing a web page for the BookTech application. This website will have a listing of books and their details.

Creating Templates

Overview

In our BookTech application, we've created models for Book, Author, and Publisher to manage our data. We've set up views and URL routing to display lists of books and detailed information for individual books. We also explored handling forms to add new books and used decorators to enhance view functionality. We will focus on creating templates to render our data as HTML, providing a user-friendly interface for our application.

Django templates are HTML files that allow you to generate dynamic web pages by embedding Django template language (DTL) syntax. Templates enable you to separate the presentation layer from the business logic, making your code more maintainable and easier to manage. Templates can include variables, logic (like loops and conditionals), and filters to format data before rendering.

Setting up Django Templates

Configure Template Settings

First, ensure that your Django project is configured to use templates. Open your settings.py file and check that the TEMPLATES setting includes the correct directory for your templates:

```
TEMPLATES = [
    {
        'BACKEND':
'django.template.backends.django.DjangoTemplates',
        'DIRS': [os.path.join(BASE_DIR, 'templates')],
        'APP_DIRS': True,
        'OPTIONS': {
            'context_processors': [

'django.template.context_processors.debug',

'django.template.context_processors.request',

'django.contrib.auth.context_processors.auth',

'django.contrib.messages.context_processors.messages',
            ],
        },
    },
]
```

This configuration tells Django to look for templates in the templates directory at the project root and within each app.

Create Template Directory

Create a templates directory at the root of your project and within the library app:

```
mkdir templates

mkdir -p library/templates/library
```

Create a Base Template

A base template provides a common structure that other templates can extend. This promotes reusability and consistency across your site.

Create a file named base.html in the templates directory:

```
<!DOCTYPE html>

<html>

<head>

    <title>{% block title %}BookTech{% endblock
%}</title>

    <link rel="stylesheet" type="text/css" href="{%
static 'styles.css' %}">

</head>

<body>

    <header>

        <h1>BookTech</h1>

        <nav>

            <ul>

                <li><a href="{% url 'book_list'
%}">Home</a></li>
```

```
                    <li><a href="{% url 'add_book' %}">Add
Book</a></li>
                </ul>
            </nav>
        </header>
        <main>
            {% block content %}{% endblock %}
        </main>
        <footer>
            <p>&copy; 2024 BookTech</p>
        </footer>
</body>
</html>
```

This template includes placeholders for the title and content, which can be overridden by child templates.

Create Child Templates

- Book List Template

Create a file named book_list.html in library/templates/library:

```
{% extends 'base.html' %}


{% block title %}Book List{% endblock %}
```

```
{% block content %}

    <h2>Book List</h2>

    <ul>

        {% for book in books %}

            <li><a href="{% url 'book_detail' book.id
%}">{{ book.title }}</a> by {{ book.author.first_name }}
{{ book.author.last_name }}</li>

        {% endfor %}

    </ul>

{% endblock %}
```

This template extends base.html and overrides the title and content blocks to display the list of books.

- Book Detail Template

Create a file named book_detail.html in library/templates/library:

```
{% extends 'base.html' %}


{% block title %}{{ book.title }}{% endblock %}


{% block content %}

    <h2>{{ book.title }}</h2>

    <p><strong>Author:</strong> {{ book.author.first_name
}} {{ book.author.last_name }}</p>
```

```
    <p><strong>Publication Date:</strong> {{
book.publication_date }}</p>

    <p><strong>ISBN:</strong> {{ book.isbn }}</p>

    <p><strong>Publishers:</strong>

        <ul>

            {% for publisher in book.publishers.all %}

                <li>{{ publisher.name }}</li>

            {% endfor %}

        </ul>

    </p>

    <p><a href="{% url 'book_list' %}">Back to book
list</a></p>

{% endblock %}
```

This template extends base.html and overrides the title and content blocks to display detailed information about a specific book.

Update Views to Use Templates

Ensure your views in library/views.py render the appropriate templates:

```
from django.shortcuts import render, get_object_or_404

from .models import Book


def book_list(request):

    books = Book.objects.all()
```

```
    return render(request, 'library/book_list.html',
{'books': books})


def book_detail(request, book_id):

    book = get_object_or_404(Book, id=book_id)

    return render(request, 'library/book_detail.html',
{'book': book})
```

After you launch the server, navigate to following URLs to test the templates:

- http://127.0.0.1:8000/library/books/ to see the list of books.
- http://127.0.0.1:8000/library/books/1/ to see the details of the book with ID 1.

Styling with CSS

You can add a CSS file to style your templates. Create a static directory at the root of your project and within the library app:

```
mkdir static

mkdir -p library/static/library
```

Create a CSS file named styles.css in the static directory:

```
body {

    font-family: Arial, sans-serif;

    margin: 0;

    padding: 0;

    background-color: #f4f4f4;

}
```

```
header {
    background-color: #333;
    color: white;
    padding: 10px 0;
    text-align: center;
}

nav ul {
    list-style: none;
    padding: 0;
}

nav ul li {
    display: inline;
    margin: 0 10px;
}

nav ul li a {
    color: white;
    text-decoration: none;
}
```

```
main {
    padding: 20px;
}

footer {
    background-color: #333;
    color: white;
    text-align: center;
    padding: 10px 0;
    position: fixed;
    bottom: 0;
    width: 100%;
}
```

Ensure your base template includes the link to the static CSS file:

```
<head>
    <title>{% block title %}BookTech{% endblock
%}</title>
    <link rel="stylesheet" type="text/css" href="{%
static 'styles.css' %}">
</head>
```

Update your settings.py to include the static files settings:

```
STATIC_URL = '/static/'
```

The front end of your web app can be built in a way that is both scalable and easy to maintain by following these steps. You have also created a base template for consistency and child templates to extend it.

Template Tags and Filters

Overview

Django template tags and filters are powerful tools that allow you to add logic and formatting to your templates. Tags provide functionalities like loops, conditionals, and including other templates, while filters help format data by transforming it in various ways. Django comes with a variety of built-in tags and filters, and you can also create custom ones to suit your specific needs.

Built-in Template Tags

{% for %}

Used to loop over a sequence of items:

```
{% for book in books %}

    <li>{{ book.title }}</li>

{% endfor %}
```

{% if %}

Used for conditional statements:

```
{% if books %}

    <ul>

    {% for book in books %}

        <li>{{ book.title }}</li>
```

```
    {% endfor %}
    </ul>
{% else %}
    <p>No books available.</p>
{% endif %}
```

{% block %} and {% extends %}

Used for template inheritance:

```
{% extends 'base.html' %}


{% block content %}
    <h1>Book List</h1>
    <ul>
    {% for book in books %}
        <li>{{ book.title }}</li>
    {% endfor %}
    </ul>
{% endblock %}
```

{% include %}

Includes another template within the current template:

```
{% include 'library/book_snippet.html' with book=book %}
```

Built-in Template Filters

Date

Formats a date:

```
{{ book.publication_date|date:"F d, Y" }}
```

Length

Returns the length of a list:

```
{{ books|length }}
```

Truncatechars

Truncates a string to a specified number of characters:

```
{{ book.description|truncatechars:100 }}
```

lower and upper

Converts a string to lowercase or uppercase:

```
{{ book.title|lower }}

{{ book.title|upper }}
```

Custom Template Tags and Filters

Custom tags and filters can be created to add specific functionality that is not covered by the built-in options.

Creating Custom Filters

Create a file named library/templatetags/library_filters.py:

```
mkdir library/templatetags

touch library/templatetags/__init__.py
```

```
touch library/templatetags/library_filters.py
```

Define a custom filter in library_filters.py:

```
from django import template


register = template.Library()


@register.filter(name='initials')
def initials(value):
    """
    Returns the initials of a name.
    """
    names = value.split()
    initials = ''.join([name[0] for name in names])
    return initials.upper()
```

This filter will return the initials of a given name.

Using Custom Filters in Templates

Ensure the custom filters are loaded in your template. Open book_list.html and add the following:

```
{% load library_filters %}


<ul>
{% for book in books %}
```

```
    <li>{{ book.title }} by {{ book.author.first_name }}
{{ book.author.last_name }} ({{
book.author.first_name|initials }}{{
book.author.last_name|initials }})</li>

{% endfor %}

</ul>
```

This will display the initials of the author's name next to the full name.

Creating Custom Tags

Create a custom tag in library/templatetags/library_tags.py:

```
from django import template


register = template.Library()


@register.simple_tag

def total_books():

    """

    Returns the total number of books.

    """

    from library.models import Book

    return Book.objects.count()
```

This tag will return the total number of books in the database.

Using Custom Tags in Templates

Load and use the custom tag in your template. Open base.html and add the following:

```
{% load library_tags %}


<footer>

    <p>&copy; 2024 BookTech - Total Books: {% total_books
%}</p>

</footer>
```

This will display the total number of books in the footer.

After you launch the server, navigate to http://127.0.0.1:8000/library/books/ to see the custom tags and filters in action. Generally speaking, the built-in tags and filters offer a powerful suite of tools that can be further customized and enhanced with custom tags and filters.

Context and Rendering

Rendering refers to the process of generating HTML from templates, while context refers to the data that is passed to templates. When a view renders a template, it combines the template with a context to produce a final HTML response. Understanding how to pass data to templates is crucial for building dynamic web applications.

Rendering Templates with Context

To render a template with context, you use the render function in Django views. The render function takes the request object, the path to the template, and a context dictionary containing the data you want to pass to the template.

We will start with a simple example. Assume you have a template hello.html:

```
<!-- templates/hello.html -->

<!DOCTYPE html>

<html>

<head>
```

```
    <title>Hello</title>
</head>
<body>
    <h1>Hello, {{ name }}!</h1>
</body>
</html>
```

You can render this template from a view and pass the name context variable:

```
from django.shortcuts import render


def hello_view(request):
    context = {'name': 'World'}
    return render(request, 'hello.html', context)
```

The context dictionary {'name': 'World'} makes the name variable available in the template.

Sample Program: Rendering Templates in BookTech

We will apply this to our BookTech application by passing data from our views to our templates. We will update the book_list and book_detail views to include additional context data.

Updating the Book List View

Open library/views.py and modify the book_list view to pass the total number of books to the template:

```
from django.shortcuts import render
from .models import Book
```

```
def book_list(request):
    books = Book.objects.all()
    total_books = books.count()
    context = {
        'books': books,
        'total_books': total_books
    }
    return render(request, 'library/book_list.html',
context)
```

Update book_list.html to display the total number of books:

```
<!-- library/templates/library/book_list.html -->
{% extends 'base.html' %}

{% block title %}Book List{% endblock %}

{% block content %}
    <h2>Book List (Total: {{ total_books }})</h2>
    <ul>
    {% for book in books %}
        <li><a href="{% url 'book_detail' book.id %}">{{
book.title }}</a> by {{ book.author.first_name }} {{
book.author.last_name }}</li>
```

```
    {% endfor %}

    </ul>

{% endblock %}
```

Updating the Book Detail View

Modify the book_detail view to include additional context data, such as the number of publishers for the book:

```
from django.shortcuts import render, get_object_or_404

from .models import Book


def book_detail(request, book_id):

    book = get_object_or_404(Book, id=book_id)

    total_publishers = book.publishers.count()

    context = {

        'book': book,

        'total_publishers': total_publishers

    }

    return render(request, 'library/book_detail.html',
context)
```

Update book_detail.html to display the total number of publishers:

```
<!-- library/templates/library/book_detail.html -->

{% extends 'base.html' %}
```

```
{% block title %}{{ book.title }}{% endblock %}


{% block content %}

    <h2>{{ book.title }}</h2>

    <p><strong>Author:</strong> {{ book.author.first_name
}} {{ book.author.last_name }}</p>

    <p><strong>Publication Date:</strong> {{
book.publication_date }}</p>

    <p><strong>ISBN:</strong> {{ book.isbn }}</p>

    <p><strong>Publishers (Total: {{ total_publishers
}}):</strong>

        <ul>

            {% for publisher in book.publishers.all %}

                <li>{{ publisher.name }}</li>

            {% endfor %}

        </ul>

    </p>

    <p><a href="{% url 'book_list' %}">Back to book
list</a></p>

{% endblock %}
```

Context Processors

Sometimes, you need to make certain context data available to all templates. Context processors are functions that add context data to every template rendering request. To use context processors, add them to the TEMPLATES setting in settings.py.

Creating a Context Processor

Create a file named library/context_processors.py:

```
from .models import Author


def authors(request):
    return {
        'authors': Author.objects.all()
    }
```

Registering the Context Processor

Add the context processor to the TEMPLATES setting in settings.py:

```
TEMPLATES = [
    {
        'BACKEND':
'django.template.backends.django.DjangoTemplates',
        'DIRS': [os.path.join(BASE_DIR, 'templates')],
        'APP_DIRS': True,
        'OPTIONS': {
            'context_processors': [

'django.template.context_processors.debug',

'django.template.context_processors.request',
```

```
'django.contrib.auth.context_processors.auth',

'django.contrib.messages.context_processors.messages',
                'library.context_processors.authors',
            ],
        },
    },
]
```

The authors context variable is now available in all templates.

Using Context Processor in Templates

Update base.html to display a list of all authors in the footer:

```
<!-- templates/base.html -->

<!DOCTYPE html>

<html>

<head>

    <title>{% block title %}BookTech{% endblock
%}</title>

    <link rel="stylesheet" type="text/css" href="{%
static 'styles.css' %}">

</head>

<body>

    <header>
```

```
        <h1>BookTech</h1>
        <nav>
            <ul>
                <li><a href="{% url 'book_list'
%}">Home</a></li>
                <li><a href="{% url 'add_book' %}">Add
Book</a></li>
            </ul>
        </nav>
    </header>
    <main>
        {% block content %}{% endblock %}
    </main>
    <footer>
        <p>&copy; 2024 BookTech</p>
        <p>Authors:</p>
        <ul>
            {% for author in authors %}
                <li>{{ author.first_name }} {{
author.last_name }}</li>
            {% endfor %}
        </ul>
```

```
    </footer>
</body>
</html>
```

The above sample program demonstrates how to pass data to templates using context and context processors, enhancing the flexibility and dynamism of your web pages.

Rendering Multiple Context Variables

You can pass multiple context variables to a template by adding them to the context dictionary:

```
def book_list(request):
    books = Book.objects.all()
    total_books = books.count()
    authors = Author.objects.all()
    context = {
        'books': books,
        'total_books': total_books,
        'authors': authors
    }
    return render(request, 'library/book_list.html',
context)
```

In your template, you can access all these variables:

```
<!-- library/templates/library/book_list.html -->
{% extends 'base.html' %}
```

```
{% block title %}Book List{% endblock %}


{% block content %}
    <h2>Book List (Total: {{ total_books }})</h2>
    <ul>
    {% for book in books %}
        <li><a href="{% url 'book_detail' book.id %}">{{
book.title }}</a> by {{ book.author.first_name }} {{
book.author.last_name }}</li>
    {% endfor %}
    </ul>
    <h3>Authors</h3>
    <ul>
    {% for author in authors %}
        <li>{{ author.first_name }} {{ author.last_name
}}</li>
    {% endfor %}
    </ul>
{% endblock %}
```

This setup allows you to create rich, data-driven web pages by efficiently passing and rendering context data within your Django templates. The ability to render multiple context variables and use context processors significantly enhances the functionality and maintainability of your application.

Hands-on Lab: Design Book Listing and Detail Page

In this hands-on task, we will design a book listing and detail page using the concepts and skills we've learned so far. We will create views, templates, and URL configurations to display a list of all books and detailed information for each book in our BookTech application.

Define the Models

Ensure that your Book, Author, and Publisher models are properly defined in library/models.py. Following is a quick recap:

```
from django.db import models


class Author(models.Model):

    first_name = models.CharField(max_length=50)

    last_name = models.CharField(max_length=50)

    birth_date = models.DateField()


    def __str__(self):

        return f"{self.first_name} {self.last_name}"


class Publisher(models.Model):

    name = models.CharField(max_length=100)

    address = models.CharField(max_length=255)

    city = models.CharField(max_length=100)

    state_province = models.CharField(max_length=100)
```

```
    country = models.CharField(max_length=100)

    website = models.URLField()


    def __str__(self):

        return self.name


class Book(models.Model):

    title = models.CharField(max_length=200)

    author = models.ForeignKey(Author,
on_delete=models.CASCADE)

    publication_date = models.DateField()

    isbn = models.CharField(max_length=17)

    publishers = models.ManyToManyField(Publisher)


    def __str__(self):

        return self.title
```

Create Views for Book List and Detail Pages

Book List View

Open library/views.py and create a function-based view to display the list of books:

```
from django.shortcuts import render

from .models import Book
```

```
def book_list(request):
    books = Book.objects.all()
    context = {
        'books': books,
        'total_books': books.count()
    }
    return render(request, 'library/book_list.html',
context)
```

Book Detail View

Create another function-based view to display the details of a specific book:

```
from django.shortcuts import render, get_object_or_404
from .models import Book


def book_detail(request, book_id):
    book = get_object_or_404(Book, id=book_id)
    context = {
        'book': book,
        'total_publishers': book.publishers.count()
    }
    return render(request, 'library/book_detail.html',
context)
```

Define URL Patterns

Update library/urls.py to include URL patterns for the book list and book detail views:

```
from django.urls import path

from . import views


urlpatterns = [

    path('books/', views.book_list, name='book_list'),

    path('books/<int:book_id>/', views.book_detail,
name='book_detail'),

]
```

Create Templates

Book List Template

Create a template to display the list of books. Create library/templates/library/book_list.html with the following content:

```
{% extends 'base.html' %}


{% block title %}Book List{% endblock %}


{% block content %}

    <h2>Book List (Total: {{ total_books }})</h2>

    <ul>

    {% for book in books %}
```

```
        <li><a href="{% url 'book_detail' book.id %}">{{
book.title }}</a> by {{ book.author.first_name }} {{
book.author.last_name }}</li>

    {% endfor %}

    </ul>

{% endblock %}
```

Book Detail Template

Create a template to display the details of a specific book.

Create library/templates/library/book_detail.html with the following content:

```
{% extends 'base.html' %}


{% block title %}{{ book.title }}{% endblock %}


{% block content %}

    <h2>{{ book.title }}</h2>

    <p><strong>Author:</strong> {{ book.author.first_name
}} {{ book.author.last_name }}</p>

    <p><strong>Publication Date:</strong> {{
book.publication_date }}</p>

    <p><strong>ISBN:</strong> {{ book.isbn }}</p>

    <p><strong>Publishers (Total: {{ total_publishers
}}):</strong>

        <ul>
```

```
            {% for publisher in book.publishers.all %}
                <li>{{ publisher.name }}</li>
            {% endfor %}
        </ul>
    </p>
    <p><a href="{% url 'book_list' %}">Back to book
list</a></p>
{% endblock %}
```

Add Sample Data

To test the views and templates, add some sample data to your database. You can use the Django admin interface or the shell to add authors, publishers, and books.

Once you've started the server, go to http://127.0.0.1:8000/admin/ and add some authors, publishers, and books.

Using Django Shell

Alternatively, you can add sample data using the Django shell:

```
python manage.py shell
```

In the shell, add some sample data:

```
from library.models import Author, Publisher, Book
from datetime import date


author1 = Author.objects.create(first_name='John',
last_name='Doe', birth_date=date(1970, 1, 1))
```

```
author2 = Author.objects.create(first_name='Jane',
last_name='Smith', birth_date=date(1980, 5, 15))


publisher1 = Publisher.objects.create(name='Tech Books
Publishing', address='123 Main St', city='New York',
state_province='NY', country='USA',
website='http://techbooks.com')

publisher2 = Publisher.objects.create(name='Knowledge Hub
Publishing', address='456 Elm St', city='San Francisco',
state_province='CA', country='USA',
website='http://knowledgehub.com')


book1 = Book.objects.create(title='Learning Django',
author=author1, publication_date=date(2020, 1, 1),
isbn='9781234567890')

book1.publishers.add(publisher1, publisher2)


book2 = Book.objects.create(title='Advanced Django',
author=author2, publication_date=date(2018, 6, 1),
isbn='9781234567891')

book2.publishers.add(publisher1)
```

Once you've started the server, go to following URLs to test the views and templates:

- http://127.0.0.1:8000/library/books/ to see the list of books.
- http://127.0.0.1:8000/library/books/1/ to see the details of the book with ID 1.

With these final touches, our BookTech application fully incorporates all of our previous learnings regarding rendering templates with context data, utilizing template tags and filters, and creating dynamic web pages, culminating in a listing and detail page design.

Summary

To summarize what we learned in this chapter, we looked at Django templates and how to utilize them to construct dynamic and visually appealing web pages. We began by configuring Django templates and learning how to generate and use them to render HTML content efficiently. We created a templates directory to keep our template files and configured the template settings in settings.py.

We looked at template inheritance and learnt how to create base templates with common parts while overriding particular areas in child templates to adapt content for individual pages. Next, we looked at template tags and filters. We learned built-in tags like {% for%}, {% if%}, {% block%}, {% extends%}, and {% include%}, which provide logic and structure to templates. We also learnt how to format data using built-in filters such as date, length, truncatechars, lower, and uppercase. In addition, we developed new tags and filters to add special functionality that was not covered by the built-in options. We then concentrated on context and rendering, which entailed sending data from views to templates via the render function. We discovered how to generate context dictionaries and how context processors make certain data available to all templates.

We concluded with a practical exercise in which we put these ideas into action by creating a BookTech application listing and detail page. To do this, we had to construct templates to show a list of books with extensive descriptions, as well as views to define URL patterns. By combining these features, we improved our grasp of Django templates and their role in creating dynamic, data-driven web applications.

Test Your Knowledge

1. What is the primary purpose of Django templates?

a) To define the structure of the database
b) To process web requests and return web responses
c) To separate the presentation layer from the business logic
d) To manage static files and media

Answer: c) To separate the presentation layer from the business logic

2. Which Django setting specifies the directories to search for templates?

a) TEMPLATES_DIRS
b) TEMPLATES_PATH
c) TEMPLATE_DIRS
d) DIRS within TEMPLATES

Answer: d) DIRS within TEMPLATES

3. How do you extend a base template in Django?

a) {% base 'base.html' %}
b) {% extend 'base.html' %}
c) {% extends 'base.html' %}
d) {% include 'base.html' %}

Answer: c) {% extends 'base.html' %}

4. Which template tag is used to include another template within a template?

a) {% import 'template.html' %}
b) {% extend 'template.html' %}
c) {% include 'template.html' %}
d) {% load 'template.html' %}

Answer: c) {% include 'template.html' %}

5. What does the {% for %} template tag do?

a) Defines a block of reusable HTML
b) Iterates over a sequence of items
c) Conditionally includes content
d) Extends a base template

Answer: b) Iterates over a sequence of items

6. How do you format a date in a Django template?

a) {{ date|format:"F d, Y" }}
b) {{ date|date:"F d, Y" }}
c) {{ date|strftime:"F d, Y" }}
d) {{ date|datetime:"F d, Y" }}

Answer: b) {{ date|date:"F d, Y" }}

7. Which filter would you use to convert a string to uppercase in a Django template?

a) {{ string|upper }}
b) {{ string|uppercase }}
c) {{ string|to_upper }}
d) {{ string|capitalize }}

Answer: a) {{ string|upper }}

8. What is the role of a context processor in Django?

a) To manage static files and media
b) To add context data to every template rendering request
c) To handle form submissions and validations
d) To define URL patterns for the application

Answer: b) To add context data to every template rendering request

9. How do you render a template with context data in a Django view?

a) return render_template(request, 'template.html', context)
b) return render(request, 'template.html', context)
c) return render_to_response('template.html', context)
d) return HttpResponse('template.html', context)

Answer: b) return render(request, 'template.html', context)

10. Which of the following correctly passes multiple context variables to a template?

a) context = {'var1': value1, 'var2': value2}
b) context = ['var1': value1, 'var2': value2]
c) context = ('var1': value1, 'var2': value2)
d) context = {"var1": value1, "var2": value2}

Answer: a) context = {'var1': value1, 'var2': value2}

CHAPTER 5: FORMS AND VALIDATION

Introduction

This chapter will teach you how to successfully manage user input in your Django apps. We will start by learning how to develop forms in Django that allow users to input data via your web application. You'll learn how to create and display forms, maintaining a consistent user experience. We will then go over form validation, which is critical for ensuring data integrity. You'll learn how Django handles basic validation automatically, as well as how you can create custom validation rules to verify that user input satisfies your application's needs.

We will also go over model forms, a useful feature that streamlines form construction by leveraging your current Django models. This strategy minimizes boilerplate code and guarantees that your forms are tightly linked to your data models. We will also look at formsets, which allow you to manage many forms on a single page, making it easier to handle complex data entry scenarios.

Finally, we will go over custom validation, in which you'll learn how to create custom logic to enforce certain validation criteria. The chapter will end with an interactive task that will help you strengthen what you have learned. You will be asked to develop and validate a book submission form for the BookTech application. This hands-on exercise will help you apply the principles and techniques you've learned to a real-world scenario, ensuring that you can properly manage user input in your Django projects.

Creating Forms

Introduction to Forms in Django

Forms are a crucial component of web applications, allowing users to submit data that can be processed and stored. Django provides a robust forms framework that simplifies the creation, validation, and processing of forms. There are primarily two types of forms in Django: regular forms and model forms. Regular forms are used to capture user input without directly tying it to a database model, while model forms are linked to Django models and automatically generate form fields based on model fields.

Building and Displaying Regular Forms

Creating a Form Class

To create a regular form, define a form class in forms.py using django.forms. For instance, we will create a form for users to submit feedback.

First, create the forms.py file in your library app if it doesn't already exist:

```
touch library/forms.py
```

Then, define the form class:

```
from django import forms


class FeedbackForm(forms.Form):

    name = forms.CharField(max_length=100, label='Your
Name')

    email = forms.EmailField(label='Your Email')

    message = forms.CharField(widget=forms.Textarea,
label='Your Feedback')
```

This class defines a form with three fields: name, email, and message.

Displaying the Form in a View

Next, create a view to handle displaying the form and processing form submissions. Open library/views.py and add the following view:

```
from django.shortcuts import render

from .forms import FeedbackForm


def feedback_view(request):

    if request.method == 'POST':

        form = FeedbackForm(request.POST)

        if form.is_valid():

            # Process the data in form.cleaned_data
```

```
            # For now, we'll just print it to the console

            print(form.cleaned_data)

            return render(request,
'library/feedback_thanks.html')

    else:

        form = FeedbackForm()

    return render(request, 'library/feedback.html',
{'form': form})
```

This view handles both displaying the form and processing the form data when submitted.

Creating Templates for the Form

Create a template to display the form. Create library/templates/library/feedback.html with the following content:

```
<!DOCTYPE html>

<html>

<head>

    <title>Feedback</title>

</head>

<body>

    <h1>Feedback Form</h1>

    <form method="post">

        {% csrf_token %}

        {{ form.as_p }}
```

```
        <button type="submit">Submit</button>

    </form>

</body>

</html>
```

This template includes the form and a submit button.

Also, create a simple thank-you template to display after form submission. Create library/templates/library/feedback_thanks.html:

```
<!DOCTYPE html>

<html>

<head>

    <title>Thank You</title>

</head>

<body>

    <h1>Thank You for Your Feedback!</h1>

</body>

</html>
```

Defining URL Patterns for the Form

Update library/urls.py to include a URL pattern for the feedback view:

```
from django.urls import path

from . import views
```

```
urlpatterns = [

    path('feedback/', views.feedback_view,
name='feedback'),

]
```

Once you've started the server, go to http://127.0.0.1:8000/feedback/ to see the feedback form. Fill out the form and submit it to test the functionality.

Building and Displaying Model Forms

Model forms are a more advanced type of form that automatically generates form fields based on the fields of a Django model. This significantly reduces the amount of code you need to write and ensures that your forms are tightly integrated with your models.

We will create a model form for the Book model. Define the form class in library/forms.py:

```
from django import forms

from .models import Book



class BookForm(forms.ModelForm):

    class Meta:

        model = Book

        fields = ['title', 'author', 'publication_date',
'isbn', 'publishers']
```

This form class uses the Book model to automatically generate form fields for title, author, publication_date, isbn, and publishers.

Displaying the Model Form in a View

Create a view to handle displaying the book form and processing form submissions. Open library/views.py and add the following view:

```python
from django.shortcuts import render, redirect

from .forms import BookForm


def add_book_view(request):

    if request.method == 'POST':

        form = BookForm(request.POST)

        if form.is_valid():

            form.save()

            return redirect('book_list')

    else:

        form = BookForm()

    return render(request, 'library/add_book.html',
{'form': form})
```

This view handles both displaying the form and saving the form data to the database when submitted.

Creating a Template for the Model Form

Create a template to display the book form. Create library/templates/library/add_book.html with the following content:

```html
<!DOCTYPE html>

<html>

<head>

    <title>Add Book</title>
```

```
</head>

<body>

    <h1>Add a New Book</h1>

    <form method="post">

        {% csrf_token %}

        {{ form.as_p }}

        <button type="submit">Add Book</button>

    </form>

</body>

</html>
```

Defining URL Patterns for the Model Form

Update library/urls.py to include a URL pattern for the add book view:

```
from django.urls import path

from . import views



urlpatterns = [

    path('books/add/', views.add_book_view,
name='add_book'),

]
```

Then go to http://127.0.0.1:8000/books/add/ to see the book form. Fill out the form and submit it to test the functionality. Your web projects will be more interactive and functional if you know how to make and show model forms in addition to regular ones. This will allow you to take user input in Django applications and process it effectively.

Form Validation

Form validation ensures that the data submitted through forms meets certain criteria before it is processed or saved. This is crucial for maintaining data integrity and preventing invalid or harmful data from entering your system. Django provides a robust mechanism for validating form data, both through built-in validation and custom validation logic.

Built-in Validation

Django automatically handles basic validation for form fields based on the field types. For example, if you define a CharField with a maximum length, Django ensures that the input does not exceed this length. Similarly, an EmailField will only accept valid email addresses.

Basic Form with Built-in Validation

We will create a simple form to demonstrate built-in validation. Assume we have the following FeedbackForm in library/forms.py:

```
from django import forms


class FeedbackForm(forms.Form):

    name = forms.CharField(max_length=100, label='Your
Name')

    email = forms.EmailField(label='Your Email')

    message = forms.CharField(widget=forms.Textarea,
label='Your Feedback')
```

The CharField for name ensures that the name does not exceed 100 characters, and the EmailField ensures the email is valid.

Displaying Validation Errors

When the form is submitted, Django automatically validates the data. If there are any errors, they are stored in the form's errors attribute, which you can display in your template.

Update the feedback_view in library/views.py to handle form validation:

```
from django.shortcuts import render
from .forms import FeedbackForm

def feedback_view(request):
    if request.method == 'POST':
        form = FeedbackForm(request.POST)
        if form.is_valid():
            # Process the data in form.cleaned_data
            print(form.cleaned_data)
            return render(request,
'library/feedback_thanks.html')
    else:
        form = FeedbackForm()
    return render(request, 'library/feedback.html',
{'form': form})
```

Update the feedback.html template to display form errors:

```
<!DOCTYPE html>
<html>
<head>
    <title>Feedback</title>
</head>
<body>
```

```
    <h1>Feedback Form</h1>

    <form method="post">

        {% csrf_token %}

        {{ form.as_p }}

        {% if form.errors %}

            <ul>

            {% for field in form %}

                {% if field.errors %}

                    <li>{{ field.name }}: {{ field.errors
}}</li>

                {% endif %}

            {% endfor %}

            </ul>

        {% endif %}

        <button type="submit">Submit</button>

    </form>

</body>

</html>
```

This will display any validation errors next to the corresponding fields.

Custom Validation

In addition to built-in validation, Django allows you to define custom validation rules for your forms. You can do this by overriding the clean method for individual fields or the clean method for the entire form.

Custom Field Validation

To add custom validation for a specific field, override the clean_<fieldname> method in your form class. For example, we will ensure that the name field does not contain any numbers:

```
from django import forms


class FeedbackForm(forms.Form):

    name = forms.CharField(max_length=100, label='Your
Name')

    email = forms.EmailField(label='Your Email')

    message = forms.CharField(widget=forms.Textarea,
label='Your Feedback')


    def clean_name(self):

        name = self.cleaned_data.get('name')

        if any(char.isdigit() for char in name):

            raise forms.ValidationError('Name cannot
contain numbers.')

        return name
```

This method checks if the name field contains any digits and raises a ValidationError if it does.

Custom Form-wide Validation

To add custom validation that involves multiple fields, override the clean method for the entire form. For example, we will ensure that the message field is at least 10 characters long:

```
from django import forms
```

```
class FeedbackForm(forms.Form):

    name = forms.CharField(max_length=100, label='Your
Name')

    email = forms.EmailField(label='Your Email')

    message = forms.CharField(widget=forms.Textarea,
label='Your Feedback')


    def clean(self):

        cleaned_data = super().clean()

        message = cleaned_data.get('message')

        if message and len(message) < 10:

            self.add_error('message', 'Message must be at
least 10 characters long.')

        return cleaned_data
```

This method checks the length of the message field and adds an error if it is too short.

Validating Model Forms

Model forms benefit from built-in validation based on the model fields' definitions, but you can also add custom validation logic.

Custom Validation in Model Forms

We will update the BookForm to ensure that the isbn field contains exactly 13 characters:

```
from django import forms

from .models import Book
```

```
class BookForm(forms.ModelForm):
    class Meta:
        model = Book
        fields = ['title', 'author', 'publication_date',
'isbn', 'publishers']

    def clean_isbn(self):
        isbn = self.cleaned_data.get('isbn')
        if len(isbn) != 13:
            raise forms.ValidationError('ISBN must be
exactly 13 characters long.')
        return isbn
```

Using the Validated Model Form

Ensure your view and template handle displaying any validation errors:

```
from django.shortcuts import render, redirect
from .forms import BookForm

def add_book_view(request):
    if request.method == 'POST':
        form = BookForm(request.POST)
        if form.is_valid():
            form.save()
```

```
            return redirect('book_list')
    else:
        form = BookForm()
    return render(request, 'library/add_book.html',
{'form': form})
```

Update the add_book.html template to display errors:

```
<!DOCTYPE html>
<html>
<head>
    <title>Add Book</title>
</head>
<body>
    <h1>Add a New Book</h1>
    <form method="post">
        {% csrf_token %}
        {{ form.as_p }}
        {% if form.errors %}
            <ul>
            {% for field in form %}
                {% if field.errors %}
                    <li>{{ field.name }}: {{ field.errors
}}</li>
```

```
                {% endif %}

            {% endfor %}

            </ul>

        {% endif %}

        <button type="submit">Add Book</button>

    </form>

</body>

</html>
```

With this, you can make sure user input is clean, consistent, and follows the rules your application defines.

Model Forms

Overview

Model forms in Django provide a convenient way to create forms directly from your models. This ensures that your forms are closely tied to your database schema, reducing redundancy and the likelihood of errors. By using model forms, you can automatically generate form fields based on your model's fields, complete with built-in validation according to the model's field definitions.

Creating Model Forms

Defining a Model Form

We will create a model form for the Book model in our BookTech application. This model form will automatically include fields for title, author, publication_date, isbn, and publishers.

First, ensure your Book model is defined in library/models.py:

```
from django.db import models

class Author(models.Model):
```

```
    first_name = models.CharField(max_length=50)
    last_name = models.CharField(max_length=50)
    birth_date = models.DateField()

    def __str__(self):
        return f"{self.first_name} {self.last_name}"

class Publisher(models.Model):
    name = models.CharField(max_length=100)
    address = models.CharField(max_length=255)
    city = models.CharField(max_length=100)
    state_province = models.CharField(max_length=100)
    country = models.CharField(max_length=100)
    website = models.URLField()

    def __str__(self):
        return self.name

class Book(models.Model):
    title = models.CharField(max_length=200)
    author = models.ForeignKey(Author,
on_delete=models.CASCADE)
```

```
    publication_date = models.DateField()
    isbn = models.CharField(max_length=17)
    publishers = models.ManyToManyField(Publisher)

    def __str__(self):
        return self.title
```

Next, define the model form in library/forms.py:

```
from django import forms
from .models import Book

class BookForm(forms.ModelForm):
    class Meta:
        model = Book
        fields = ['title', 'author', 'publication_date',
'isbn', 'publishers']

    def clean_isbn(self):
        isbn = self.cleaned_data.get('isbn')
        if len(isbn) != 13:
            raise forms.ValidationError('ISBN must be
exactly 13 characters long.')
```

```
        return isbn
```

This form class uses the Book model to automatically generate form fields. It also includes custom validation for the isbn field, ensuring it is exactly 13 characters long.

Displaying the Model Form in a View

Create a view to handle displaying the form and processing form submissions. Open library/views.py and add the following view:

```
from django.shortcuts import render, redirect

from .forms import BookForm


def add_book_view(request):

    if request.method == 'POST':

        form = BookForm(request.POST)

        if form.is_valid():

            form.save()

            return redirect('book_list')

    else:

        form = BookForm()

    return render(request, 'library/add_book.html',
{'form': form})
```

This view handles both displaying the form and saving the form data to the database when submitted.

Creating a Template for the Model Form

Create a template to display the book form. Create library/templates/library/add_book.html with the following content:

```
<!DOCTYPE html>
<html>
<head>
    <title>Add Book</title>
</head>
<body>
    <h1>Add a New Book</h1>
    <form method="post">
        {% csrf_token %}
        {{ form.as_p }}
        {% if form.errors %}
            <ul>
            {% for field in form %}
                {% if field.errors %}
                    <li>{{ field.name }}: {{ field.errors
}}</li>
                {% endif %}
            {% endfor %}
            </ul>
        {% endif %}
        <button type="submit">Add Book</button>
    </form>
```

```
</body>

</html>
```

Defining URL Patterns for the Model Form

Update library/urls.py to include a URL pattern for the add book view:

```
from django.urls import path

from . import views



urlpatterns = [

    path('books/add/', views.add_book_view,
name='add_book'),

]
```

Then, navigate to http://127.0.0.1:8000/books/add/ to see the book form. Fill out the form and submit it to test the functionality.

Customizing Model Forms

You can customize model forms to add widgets, labels, and initial values to the fields. We will enhance our BookForm by adding custom labels and widgets.

Customizing Form Fields

Update the BookForm in library/forms.py to include custom widgets and labels:

```
from django import forms

from .models import Book



class BookForm(forms.ModelForm):
```

```
    class Meta:
        model = Book
        fields = ['title', 'author', 'publication_date',
'isbn', 'publishers']
        widgets = {
            'publication_date':
forms.DateInput(attrs={'type': 'date'}),
        }
        labels = {
            'title': 'Book Title',
            'author': 'Author',
            'publication_date': 'Publication Date',
            'isbn': 'ISBN',
            'publishers': 'Publishers',
        }

    def clean_isbn(self):
        isbn = self.cleaned_data.get('isbn')
        if len(isbn) != 13:
            raise forms.ValidationError('ISBN must be
exactly 13 characters long.')
        return isbn
```

This customization adds a date input widget for the publication_date field and custom labels for all fields.

Displaying the Customized Model Form

Ensure your view and template handle displaying the customized form:

```
from django.shortcuts import render, redirect

from .forms import BookForm


def add_book_view(request):

    if request.method == 'POST':

        form = BookForm(request.POST)

        if form.is_valid():

            form.save()

            return redirect('book_list')

    else:

        form = BookForm()

    return render(request, 'library/add_book.html',
{'form': form})

<!DOCTYPE html>

<html>

<head>

    <title>Add Book</title>

</head>
```

```
<body>
    <h1>Add a New Book</h1>
    <form method="post">
        {% csrf_token %}
        {{ form.as_p }}
        {% if form.errors %}
            <ul>
            {% for field in form %}
                {% if field.errors %}
                    <li>{{ field.name }}: {{ field.errors
}}</li>
                {% endif %}
            {% endfor %}
            </ul>
        {% endif %}
        <button type="submit">Add Book</button>
    </form>
</body>
</html>
```

Then, navigate to http://127.0.0.1:8000/books/add/. Fill out the form and submit it to see the customized labels and widgets in action.

Thus, you can simplify your code, simplify the process of creating forms, and aid in maintaining data integrity across your application by using these model forms. This will also reduce redundancy.

Custom Validation

While Django's built-in validation covers many common use cases, there are situations where you need custom validation logic to ensure that the data submitted through your forms meets specific requirements. Custom validation can be added to individual fields or the entire form.

Custom Validation for Individual Fields

To add custom validation to individual fields, you override the clean_<fieldname> method in your form class. This method is called when the form is validated, and it allows you to add custom logic to check the validity of the field's value.

We've already seen a simple example of custom validation for the isbn field in our BookForm. We will enhance it by ensuring the ISBN consists only of digits and has exactly 13 characters.

Update the BookForm in library/forms.py:

```
from django import forms

from .models import Book


class BookForm(forms.ModelForm):

    class Meta:

        model = Book

        fields = ['title', 'author', 'publication_date',
'isbn', 'publishers']

        widgets = {

            'publication_date':
forms.DateInput(attrs={'type': 'date'}),

        }

        labels = {
```

```
            'title': 'Book Title',
            'author': 'Author',
            'publication_date': 'Publication Date',
            'isbn': 'ISBN',
            'publishers': 'Publishers',
        }

    def clean_isbn(self):
        isbn = self.cleaned_data.get('isbn')
        if not isbn.isdigit() or len(isbn) != 13:
            raise forms.ValidationError('ISBN must be
exactly 13 digits long.')
        return isbn
```

This method checks if the isbn consists only of digits and is exactly 13 characters long. If not, it raises a ValidationError.

Custom Validation for Multiple Fields

To validate the form as a whole, or to perform validation that depends on multiple fields, you override the clean method. This method allows you to add custom logic that checks the validity of the entire form's data.

We will add a validation rule to ensure that the publication_date is not in the future. Update the BookForm in library/forms.py:

```
from django import forms
from django.core.exceptions import ValidationError
from .models import Book
```

```
from datetime import date

class BookForm(forms.ModelForm):
    class Meta:
        model = Book
        fields = ['title', 'author', 'publication_date',
'isbn', 'publishers']
        widgets = {
            'publication_date':
forms.DateInput(attrs={'type': 'date'}),
        }
        labels = {
            'title': 'Book Title',
            'author': 'Author',
            'publication_date': 'Publication Date',
            'isbn': 'ISBN',
            'publishers': 'Publishers',
        }

    def clean_isbn(self):
        isbn = self.cleaned_data.get('isbn')
        if not isbn.isdigit() or len(isbn) != 13:
```

```
            raise forms.ValidationError('ISBN must be
exactly 13 digits long.')

        return isbn


    def clean(self):

        cleaned_data = super().clean()

        publication_date =
cleaned_data.get('publication_date')

        if publication_date and publication_date >
date.today():

            self.add_error('publication_date',
'Publication date cannot be in the future.')

        return cleaned_data
```

In the clean method, we check if the publication_date is in the future. If it is, we add an error to the publication_date field.

Using the Custom Validated Form

Ensure your view and template handle displaying any validation errors:

View for Handling the Custom Validated Form

Ensure your view in library/views.py looks like this:

```
from django.shortcuts import render, redirect

from .forms import BookForm



def add_book_view(request):
```

```
    if request.method == 'POST':
        form = BookForm(request.POST)
        if form.is_valid():
            form.save()
            return redirect('book_list')
    else:
        form = BookForm()
    return render(request, 'library/add_book.html',
{'form': form})
```

Template for Displaying the Custom Validated Form

Ensure your template in library/templates/library/add_book.html can display errors:

```
<!DOCTYPE html>
<html>
<head>
    <title>Add Book</title>
</head>
<body>
    <h1>Add a New Book</h1>
    <form method="post">
        {% csrf_token %}
        {{ form.as_p }}
```

```
        {% if form.errors %}
            <ul>
            {% for field in form %}
                {% if field.errors %}
                    <li>{{ field.name }}: {{ field.errors
}}</li>
                {% endif %}
            {% endfor %}
            </ul>
        {% endif %}
        <button type="submit">Add Book</button>
    </form>
</body>
</html>
```

Then, navigate to http://127.0.0.1:8000/books/add/ to test the custom validation logic. Try submitting the form with various inputs to see the validation in action.

Additional Custom Validation

You can add more complex custom validation rules based on your application's requirements. For example, you might want to ensure that the combination of title and author is unique, or that the isbn does not already exist in the database.

Ensuring Unique Combination of Title and Author

Add the following validation to the BookForm:

```
from django import forms
```

```
from django.core.exceptions import ValidationError
from .models import Book
from datetime import date


class BookForm(forms.ModelForm):
    class Meta:
        model = Book
        fields = ['title', 'author', 'publication_date',
'isbn', 'publishers']
        widgets = {
            'publication_date':
forms.DateInput(attrs={'type': 'date'}),
        }
        labels = {
            'title': 'Book Title',
            'author': 'Author',
            'publication_date': 'Publication Date',
            'isbn': 'ISBN',
            'publishers': 'Publishers',
        }

    def clean_isbn(self):
```

```
        isbn = self.cleaned_data.get('isbn')
        if not isbn.isdigit() or len(isbn) != 13:
            raise forms.ValidationError('ISBN must be
exactly 13 digits long.')
        return isbn


    def clean(self):
        cleaned_data = super().clean()
        title = cleaned_data.get('title')
        author = cleaned_data.get('author')
        publication_date =
cleaned_data.get('publication_date')
        if publication_date and publication_date >
date.today():
            self.add_error('publication_date',
'Publication date cannot be in the future.')


        # Check for unique combination of title and
author
        if title and author:
            if Book.objects.filter(title=title,
author=author).exists():
                raise forms.ValidationError('A book with
this title and author already exists.')
```

```
        return cleaned_data
```

This validation ensures that no two books with the same title and author combination exist in the database.

Summary

To start, we learned the ins and outs of making forms that can efficiently process user data. This included creating and displaying both regular and model forms. Regular forms were defined with forms.Forms and validations were handled manually. In contrast, model forms were built utilizing forms.ModelForm generates form fields depending on the Django model.

Form validation was an important topic, ensuring that data provided via forms fulfilled particular criteria. Built-in validation covered typical scenarios like field types and lengths, whereas custom validation enabled more detailed tests. For example, custom validation logic verified that an ISBN had exactly 13 digits and that publishing dates were not in the future.

In addition, we learned how to implement form-wide validation by overriding the clean function to enforce rules involving several fields. This involved implementing complicated validation criteria, such as confirming the uniqueness of a combination of fields. To put these rules into practice, we had to update the BookForm, make some changes to the views so they could process form submissions and show validation problems, and make sure the templates could really display these issues. The data within the BookTech application was kept accurate and intact because of the rigorous validation of user input that was carried out in this way.

Test Your Knowledge

1. What is the primary advantage of using model forms in Django?

a) They require less code than regular forms.
b) They automatically handle user authentication.
c) They provide built-in AJAX support.
d) They generate form fields based on the model fields and ensure consistency with the database schema.

Answer: d) They generate form fields based on the model fields and ensure consistency with the database schema.

2. Which method is used to add custom validation for a specific field in a form?

a) validate_<fieldname>

b) clean_<fieldname>
c) check_<fieldname>
d) verify_<fieldname>

Answer: b) clean_<fieldname>

3. How do you add custom validation for the entire form in Django?

a) By overriding the is_valid method
b) By defining a validate method
c) By overriding the clean method
d) By defining a check method

Answer: c) By overriding the clean method

4. Which field type ensures that only valid email addresses can be entered?

a) forms.CharField
b) forms.EmailField
c) forms.TextField
d) forms.URLField

Answer: b) forms.EmailField

5. What does the form.is_valid() method do?

a) Saves the form data to the database
b) Checks if the form data meets the validation criteria
c) Renders the form as HTML
d) Submits the form via AJAX

Answer: b) Checks if the form data meets the validation criteria

6. How do you display form validation errors in a Django template?

a) By checking form.cleaned_data
b) By using the form.errors attribute
c) By defining an error_messages dictionary
d) By calling the form.validate() method

Answer: b) By using the form.errors attribute

7. Which attribute in the form's Meta class specifies the model associated with a model form?

a) model_class
b) model
c) model_name
d) model_instance

Answer: b) model

8. What is the purpose of the widgets attribute in a form's Meta class?

a) To define custom validation rules for the form fields
b) To specify custom HTML attributes for the form fields
c) To automatically populate form fields with data
d) To list the form fields to be included in the form

Answer: b) To specify custom HTML attributes for the form fields

9. Which of the following methods would you override to add a custom validation rule that ensures a publication date is not in the future?

a) clean_publication_date
b) validate_publication_date
c) check_publication_date
d) verify_publication_date

Answer: a) clean_publication_date

10. How do you ensure that a combination of fields (e.g., title and author) is unique in a model form?

a) By using the unique_together option in the model's Meta class
b) By overriding the form's clean method and checking the combination
c) By defining a custom form field validator
d) By using the unique_combination option in the form's Meta class

CHAPTER 6: USER AUTHENTICATION AND AUTHORIZATION

Introduction

This chapter will teach you how to manage user accounts and secure Django applications. We will start with user administration, which includes how to set up user registration and authentication. This includes designing user signup forms and managing backend logic to securely store user data. Next, we will look at creating secure login and logout capabilities. You'll learn how to construct views and templates for logging users in and out, ensuring that only authenticated users have access to specific areas of your application.

Password management is another important topic, and we will go over how to handle password changes and resets safely. You will learn how to design features that allow users to update their passwords and reset them if they are forgotten, thereby improving the user experience and ensuring security. We will also look at controlling user rights and groups, which gives you control over what various users can do in your application. You'll learn how to apply rights to specific individuals or groups, allowing for more precise access control. In addition, we will go over how to enhance the default user model by constructing custom models. This enables you to add additional features and functionality according to your application's requirements.

To round off the chapter, you'll work on an interactive project that will put what you've learned about user authentication and authorization management into practice in your Django applications. You'll create a user profile and an access control system.

User Management

Django for User Management

Django provides robust built-in capabilities for user management, making it easy to handle user registration, authentication, and profile management. The Django authentication framework includes tools and views for managing user accounts, passwords, and permissions. It supports functionalities such as user login, logout, password change, password reset, and more. Django's User model comes with fields like username, email, password, first name, and last name, which can be extended as needed. This framework also provides authentication backends that you can customize to implement various authentication schemes.

Setting up User Registration and Authentication

Creating the User Registration Form

First, create a form for user registration. In library/forms.py, add the following:

```
from django import forms
```

```
from django.contrib.auth.models import User
from django.contrib.auth.forms import UserCreationForm


class UserRegistrationForm(UserCreationForm):
    email = forms.EmailField(required=True)


    class Meta:
        model = User
        fields = ['username', 'email', 'password1',
'password2']
```

This form extends UserCreationForm to include an email field, along with the default fields for username and passwords.

Creating the User Registration View

Next, create a view to handle user registration. In library/views.py, add the following:

```
from django.shortcuts import render, redirect
from .forms import UserRegistrationForm
from django.contrib.auth import login, authenticate


def register(request):
    if request.method == 'POST':
        form = UserRegistrationForm(request.POST)
        if form.is_valid():
```

```
            user = form.save()

            user.refresh_from_db()  # Load the profile
instance created by the signal

            user.save()

            raw_password =
form.cleaned_data.get('password1')

            user = authenticate(username=user.username,
password=raw_password)

            login(request, user)

            return redirect('book_list')

    else:

        form = UserRegistrationForm()

    return render(request, 'library/register.html',
{'form': form})
```

This view processes the registration form. If the form is valid, it saves the new user, logs them in, and redirects them to the book list page.

Creating the Registration Template

Create a template for the registration form. In library/templates/library/register.html, add the following:

```
<!DOCTYPE html>

<html>

<head>

    <title>Register</title>

</head>
```

```
<body>
    <h2>Register</h2>
    <form method="post">
        {% csrf_token %}
        {{ form.as_p }}
        <button type="submit">Register</button>
    </form>
</body>
</html>
```

Updating URLs

Add a URL pattern for the registration view. Update library/urls.py:

```
from django.urls import path
from . import views

urlpatterns = [
    path('register/', views.register, name='register'),
]
```

Creating the Login View

Django provides built-in views for login and logout. We will use these built-in views to handle user authentication.

First, create a template for the login form. In library/templates/registration/login.html, add the following:

```
<!DOCTYPE html>

<html>

<head>

    <title>Login</title>

</head>

<body>

    <h2>Login</h2>

    <form method="post" action="{% url 'login' %}">

        {% csrf_token %}

        {{ form.as_p }}

        <button type="submit">Login</button>

    </form>

</body>

</html>
```

Ensure you have the following setting in your settings.py to specify the login redirect URL:

```
LOGIN_REDIRECT_URL = 'book_list'
```

Add the URLs for login and logout to your project's urls.py (usually BookTech/urls.py):

```
from django.contrib.auth import views as auth_views


urlpatterns = [

    path('admin/', admin.site.urls),
```

```
    path('library/', include('library.urls')),

    path('accounts/login/',
auth_views.LoginView.as_view(), name='login'),

    path('accounts/logout/',
auth_views.LogoutView.as_view(), name='logout'),

]
```

Creating a Logout View

The logout view is handled by Django's built-in view. Ensure you have a logout template to provide feedback to the user. Create library/templates/registration/logged_out.html:

```
<!DOCTYPE html>

<html>

<head>

    <title>Logout</title>

</head>

<body>

    <h2>You have been logged out.</h2>

    <p><a href="{% url 'login' %}">Login again</a></p>

</body>

</html>
```

Then, visit http://127.0.0.1:8000/register/ to register a new user. After registration, log out and navigate to http://127.0.0.1:8000/accounts/login/ to log in with the newly created user credentials.

We have successfully implemented a basic system for user registration and authentication for your BookTech application. Among these tasks is the provision of templates for user registration forms, the handling of login and logout via Django's built-in views, and similar operations.

Login, Logout and Password Management

In the previous sections, we've touched upon setting up user registration and basic authentication. Here, we will delve deeper into implementing secure login and logout functionality in our BookTech application. This involves creating views, forms, templates, and configuring URL patterns to ensure users can log in and log out securely.

Setting up the Login Functionality

Creating the Login View

Django provides a built-in login view, but you need to configure it to match your application's needs. We will use LoginView from django.contrib.auth.views.

First, ensure the LoginView is correctly set up in your urls.py. Update your BookTech/urls.py file:

```
from django.contrib import admin

from django.urls import path, include

from django.contrib.auth import views as auth_views


urlpatterns = [

    path('admin/', admin.site.urls),

    path('library/', include('library.urls')),

    path('accounts/login/',
auth_views.LoginView.as_view(template_name='registration/
login.html'), name='login'),

    path('accounts/logout/',
auth_views.LogoutView.as_view(), name='logout'),

]
```

The LoginView is configured to use a template named registration/login.html.

Creating the Login Template

Next, create the template for the login form. In library/templates/registration/login.html, add the following content:

```
<!DOCTYPE html>

<html>

<head>

    <title>Login</title>

</head>

<body>

    <h2>Login</h2>

    <form method="post" action="{% url 'login' %}">

        {% csrf_token %}

        {{ form.as_p }}

        <button type="submit">Login</button>

    </form>

    <p>Don't have an account? <a href="{% url 'register'
%}">Register here</a></p>

</body>

</html>
```

This template includes a CSRF token for security and renders the login form fields. It also provides a link to the registration page for users who don't have an account yet.

Configuring the Login Redirect URL

Ensure you have the LOGIN_REDIRECT_URL setting in your settings.py to specify where users are redirected after logging in:

```
LOGIN_REDIRECT_URL = 'book_list'
```

This setting ensures that after a successful login, users are redirected to the book list page.

Setting up the Logout Functionality

Creating the Logout Template

Create a template to inform users that they have been logged out.

In library/templates/registration/logged_out.html, add the following content:

```
<!DOCTYPE html>

<html>

<head>

    <title>Logout</title>

</head>

<body>

    <h2>You have been logged out.</h2>

    <p><a href="{% url 'login' %}">Login again</a></p>

</body>

</html>
```

This template provides a message indicating that the user has been logged out and offers a link to log back in.

Adding Links to Login and Logout

To make it easy for users to access the login and logout functionality, add links to these actions in your base template or navigation bar.

Updating the Base Template

Modify templates/base.html to include links to login and logout. Update it as follows:

```
<!DOCTYPE html>

<html>

<head>

    <title>{% block title %}BookTech{% endblock
%}</title>

    <link rel="stylesheet" type="text/css" href="{%
static 'styles.css' %}">

</head>

<body>

    <header>

        <h1>BookTech</h1>

        <nav>

            <ul>

                <li><a href="{% url 'book_list'
%}">Home</a></li>

                <li><a href="{% url 'add_book' %}">Add
Book</a></li>

                {% if user.is_authenticated %}

                    <li><a href="{% url 'logout'
%}">Logout</a></li>

                {% else %}
```

```
                    <li><a href="{% url 'login'
%}">Login</a></li>
                    <li><a href="{% url 'register'
%}">Register</a></li>
                {% endif %}
            </ul>
        </nav>
    </header>
    <main>
        {% block content %}{% endblock %}
    </main>
    <footer>
        <p>&copy; 2024 BookTech</p>
    </footer>
</body>
</html>
```

This modification checks if the user is authenticated. If they are, it shows a logout link; otherwise, it shows links to login and register.

Navigate to http://127.0.0.1:8000/accounts/login/ to log in. Enter your credentials and log in to ensure you are redirected to the book list page. Once logged in, you should see a logout link in the navigation bar. Click the logout link to log out and verify that you are redirected to the logout page.

Password Management

In addition to login and logout, managing passwords is an essential part of user authentication. Django provides built-in views for password change and password reset as below:

Password Change

Update your urls.py to include URLs for password change:

```
from django.contrib.auth import views as auth_views


urlpatterns = [

    path('admin/', admin.site.urls),

    path('library/', include('library.urls')),

    path('accounts/login/',
auth_views.LoginView.as_view(template_name='registration/
login.html'), name='login'),

    path('accounts/logout/',
auth_views.LogoutView.as_view(), name='logout'),

    path('accounts/password_change/',
auth_views.PasswordChangeView.as_view(template_name='regi
stration/password_change_form.html'),
name='password_change'),

    path('accounts/password_change/done/',
auth_views.PasswordChangeDoneView.as_view(template_name='
registration/password_change_done.html'),
name='password_change_done'),

]
```

Create templates for the password change process.

First, create library/templates/registration/password_change_form.html:

```
<!DOCTYPE html>

<html>
```

```
<head>
    <title>Change Password</title>
</head>
<body>
    <h2>Change Password</h2>
    <form method="post">
        {% csrf_token %}
        {{ form.as_p }}
        <button type="submit">Change Password</button>
    </form>
</body>
</html>
```

Then, create library/templates/registration/password_change_done.html:

```
<!DOCTYPE html>
<html>
<head>
    <title>Password Changed</title>
</head>
<body>
    <h2>Password Change Successful</h2>
    <p>Your password has been changed successfully.</p>
```

```
    <p><a href="{% url 'book_list' %}">Return to
Home</a></p>

</body>

</html>
```

Password Reset

Update your urls.py to include URLs for password reset:

```
urlpatterns += [

    path('accounts/password_reset/',
auth_views.PasswordResetView.as_view(template_name='regis
tration/password_reset_form.html'),
name='password_reset'),

    path('accounts/password_reset/done/',
auth_views.PasswordResetDoneView.as_view(template_name='r
egistration/password_reset_done.html'),
name='password_reset_done'),

    path('accounts/reset/<uidb64>/<token>/',
auth_views.PasswordResetConfirmView.as_view(template_name
='registration/password_reset_confirm.html'),
name='password_reset_confirm'),

    path('accounts/reset/done/',
auth_views.PasswordResetCompleteView.as_view(template_nam
e='registration/password_reset_complete.html'),
name='password_reset_complete'),

]
```

Create templates for the password reset process.

Start with library/templates/registration/password_reset_form.html:

```
<!DOCTYPE html>
<html>
<head>
    <title>Reset Password</title>
</head>
<body>
    <h2>Reset Password</h2>
    <form method="post">
        {% csrf_token %}
        {{ form.as_p }}
        <button type="submit">Reset Password</button>
    </form>
</body>
</html>
```

Then, create library/templates/registration/password_reset_done.html:

```
<!DOCTYPE html>
<html>
<head>
    <title>Password Reset Sent</title>
</head>
<body>
```

```
    <h2>Password Reset Email Sent</h2>
    <p>We've emailed you instructions for setting your
password.</p>
    <p><a href="{% url 'login' %}">Return to
Login</a></p>
</body>
</html>
```

Next, create library/templates/registration/password_reset_confirm.html:

```
<!DOCTYPE html>
<html>
<head>
    <title>Set New Password</title>
</head>
<body>
    <h2>Set New Password</h2>
    <form method="post">
        {% csrf_token %}
        {{ form.as_p }}
        <button type="submit">Set New Password</button>
    </form>
</body>
```

```
</html>
```

Finally, create library/templates/registration/password_reset_complete.html:

```
<!DOCTYPE html>

<html>

<head>

    <title>Password Reset Complete</title>

</head>

<body>

    <h2>Password Reset Complete</h2>

    <p>Your password has been set. You can now log in
with your new password.</p>

    <p><a href="{% url 'login' %}">Return to
Login</a></p>

</body>

</html>
```

Your BookTech application now has secure login and logout functionality. To top it all off, you've enabled password management features like changing and resetting passwords, which gives your Django app full protection against unauthorized access.

Permissions and Groups

Managing User Permissions

The permissions are a way to control access to different parts of your application. Each user can be assigned specific permissions that determine what actions they can perform. Django provides three default permissions for each model: add, change, and delete. You can also define custom permissions.

Assigning Permissions to Users

You can assign permissions to users using the Django admin interface. We will create a user and assign permissions.

First, create a superuser to access the admin interface:

```
python manage.py createsuperuser
```

Then, log in to the Django admin interface at http://127.0.0.1:8000/admin/ and navigate to the user you want to assign permissions to. In the user's permissions section, you can select the specific permissions you want to assign.

Checking Permissions in Views

Use the @permission_required decorator to restrict access to certain views based on permissions. For example, restrict the view for adding a new book to users with the add_book permission.

In library/views.py, update the add_book_view:

```
from django.contrib.auth.decorators import
permission_required



@permission_required('library.add_book',
raise_exception=True)

def add_book_view(request):

    if request.method == 'POST':

        form = BookForm(request.POST)

        if form.is_valid():

            form.save()

            return redirect('book_list')
```

```
    else:

        form = BookForm()

    return render(request, 'library/add_book.html',
{'form': form})
```

The @permission_required decorator checks if the user has the specified permission. If not, it raises a PermissionDenied exception.

Using the has_perm Method

You can also check permissions programmatically using the has_perm method. This is useful for fine-grained control within views.

```
def add_book_view(request):

    if not request.user.has_perm('library.add_book'):

        return HttpResponseForbidden("You do not have
permission to add books.")

    if request.method == 'POST':

        form = BookForm(request.POST)

        if form.is_valid():

            form.save()

            return redirect('book_list')

    else:

        form = BookForm()

    return render(request, 'library/add_book.html',
{'form': form})
```

Managing Groups

Groups in Django are a way to manage multiple users with similar permissions. You can assign permissions to groups, and then assign users to these groups.

Creating and Managing Groups

Groups can be created and managed through the Django admin interface. Navigate to the Groups section in the admin interface and create a new group. Assign the desired permissions to the group.

Assigning Users to Groups

In the admin interface, navigate to the user you want to assign to the group. In the user's groups section, select the group you created. The user will inherit the permissions of the group.

Checking Group Membership

You can check if a user belongs to a group using the groups attribute.

```
from django.contrib.auth.models import Group


def is_member(user, group_name):

    return user.groups.filter(name=group_name).exists()
```

Use this function to check group membership within views:

```
def add_book_view(request):

    if not is_member(request.user, 'Book Managers'):

        return HttpResponseForbidden("You do not have
permission to add books.")

    if request.method == 'POST':

        form = BookForm(request.POST)

        if form.is_valid():

            form.save()
```

```
            return redirect('book_list')
    else:
        form = BookForm()
    return render(request, 'library/add_book.html',
{'form': form})
```

Advanced Group Permissions

Custom Group Permissions

Sometimes you need more complex permissions that go beyond the default add, change, and delete permissions. You can define custom permissions in your models.

In library/models.py, define custom permissions in the Meta class:

```
class Book(models.Model):
    title = models.CharField(max_length=200)
    author = models.ForeignKey(Author,
on_delete=models.CASCADE)
    publication_date = models.DateField()
    isbn = models.CharField(max_length=17)
    publishers = models.ManyToManyField(Publisher)

    class Meta:
        permissions = [
            ("can_publish_book", "Can publish book"),
        ]
```

```
    def __str__(self):
        return self.title
```

This adds a custom permission can_publish_book to the Book model.

Assigning Custom Permissions to Groups

Use the Django admin interface to assign the custom permission to a group. Navigate to the Groups section, select a group, and add the can_publish_book permission.

Checking Custom Permissions in Views

Use the @permission_required decorator or the has_perm method to check for custom permissions.

```
@permission_required('library.can_publish_book',
raise_exception=True)
def publish_book_view(request, book_id):
    book = get_object_or_404(Book, id=book_id)
    # Logic to publish the book
    return HttpResponse("Book published.")
```

Or, using the has_perm method:

```
def publish_book_view(request, book_id):
    if not
request.user.has_perm('library.can_publish_book'):
        return HttpResponseForbidden("You do not have
permission to publish books.")
    book = get_object_or_404(Book, id=book_id)
```

```
    # Logic to publish the book

    return HttpResponse("Book published.")
```

By following the instructions above, you can manage user permissions and groups. This includes the ability to assign permissions to specific individuals or groups, check permissions programmatically, and create custom permissions for more advanced access control scenarios.

Custom User Models

Necessity of Custom User Models

While Django's default User model is suitable for many applications, there are scenarios where you may need to customize it to include additional fields or functionality. Custom user models are necessary when you require:

- Extra fields for user profiles, such as a profile picture, date of birth, or bio.
- Different username field configurations, like using email as the username.
- Advanced authentication methods or additional user-related behaviors.

By creating a custom user model, you ensure that your application's user management system meets specific requirements and can evolve as needed without relying on the default limitations.

Customizing Default User Model

Creating a Custom User Model

First, define a new user model. Create or update library/models.py to include your custom user model. We will call it CustomUser.

```
from django.contrib.auth.models import AbstractBaseUser,
BaseUserManager, PermissionsMixin

from django.db import models

from django.utils.translation import ugettext_lazy as _



class CustomUserManager(BaseUserManager):
```

```
    def create_user(self, email, password=None,
**extra_fields):
        if not email:
            raise ValueError('The Email field must be
set')
        email = self.normalize_email(email)
        user = self.model(email=email, **extra_fields)
        user.set_password(password)
        user.save(using=self._db)
        return user


    def create_superuser(self, email, password=None,
**extra_fields):
        extra_fields.setdefault('is_staff', True)
        extra_fields.setdefault('is_superuser', True)
        return self.create_user(email, password,
**extra_fields)


class CustomUser(AbstractBaseUser, PermissionsMixin):
    email = models.EmailField(_('email address'),
unique=True)
    first_name = models.CharField(max_length=30,
blank=True)
```

```
    last_name = models.CharField(max_length=30,
blank=True)

    date_of_birth = models.DateField(null=True,
blank=True)

    is_active = models.BooleanField(default=True)

    is_staff = models.BooleanField(default=False)


    objects = CustomUserManager()


    USERNAME_FIELD = 'email'

    REQUIRED_FIELDS = []


    def __str__(self):

        return self.email
```

This model uses email as the username field and includes additional fields like first_name, last_name, and date_of_birth. The CustomUserManager class defines how users and superusers are created.

Updating Settings

Next, update your settings to use the custom user model. Open settings.py and add the following:

```
AUTH_USER_MODEL = 'library.CustomUser'
```

This tells Django to use the CustomUser model for authentication.

Creating User Forms

Create forms for user creation and updating. In library/forms.py, add the following:

```
from django import forms
from django.contrib.auth.forms import UserCreationForm,
UserChangeForm
from .models import CustomUser


class CustomUserCreationForm(UserCreationForm):
    class Meta:
        model = CustomUser
        fields = ('email', 'first_name', 'last_name',
'date_of_birth')


class CustomUserChangeForm(UserChangeForm):
    class Meta:
        model = CustomUser
        fields = ('email', 'first_name', 'last_name',
'date_of_birth')
```

Admin Configuration

Configure the Django admin to handle the custom user model. In library/admin.py, add the following:

```
from django.contrib import admin
from django.contrib.auth.admin import UserAdmin
from .forms import CustomUserCreationForm,
CustomUserChangeForm
```

```
from .models import CustomUser


class CustomUserAdmin(UserAdmin):
    add_form = CustomUserCreationForm
    form = CustomUserChangeForm
    model = CustomUser
    list_display = ['email', 'first_name', 'last_name',
'is_staff']
    fieldsets = (
        (None, {'fields': ('email', 'password')}),
        ('Personal info', {'fields': ('first_name',
'last_name', 'date_of_birth')}),
        ('Permissions', {'fields': ('is_active',
'is_staff', 'is_superuser', 'groups',
'user_permissions')}),
    )
    add_fieldsets = (
        (None, {
            'classes': ('wide',),
            'fields': ('email', 'password1', 'password2',
'is_staff', 'is_active')}
        ),
    )
```

```
    search_fields = ('email',)
    ordering = ('email',)


admin.site.register(CustomUser, CustomUserAdmin)
```

This configuration ensures that the admin interface can create and manage users using the custom user model.

Migrating the Database

Since we've changed the user model, we need to create and apply migrations:

```
python manage.py makemigrations
python manage.py migrate
```

Updating User Registration

Update the user registration view to use the custom user model and form. In library/views.py, modify the register view:

```
from django.shortcuts import render, redirect
from .forms import CustomUserCreationForm
from django.contrib.auth import login, authenticate


def register(request):
    if request.method == 'POST':
        form = CustomUserCreationForm(request.POST)
        if form.is_valid():
            user = form.save()
```

```
            user.refresh_from_db()  # Load the profile
instance created by the signal
            user.save()
            raw_password =
form.cleaned_data.get('password1')
            user = authenticate(username=user.email,
password=raw_password)
            login(request, user)
            return redirect('book_list')
    else:
        form = CustomUserCreationForm()
    return render(request, 'library/register.html',
{'form': form})
```

Ensure the registration template library/templates/library/register.html remains as it was previously set up, but now works with the custom user form.

Visit http://127.0.0.1:8000/register/ to register a new user with the additional fields. You should be able to register, log in, and see the new fields handled correctly.

This changes the default user model in Django to use email as the username and adds additional fields. Because of this, you were able to modify the user model to meet the requirements of your program.

Interactive Project: Build a user profile and access control system

In this hands-on practical exercise, we will apply the concepts learned so far to build a user profile and access control system for our BookTech application. We will create models for user profiles, set up views and templates to display and edit profiles, and implement an access control system using permissions and groups.

Creating the User Profile Model

Define the UserProfile Model

Extend the CustomUser model with additional profile information. Add a UserProfile model to library/models.py:

```
from django.conf import settings

from django.db import models



class UserProfile(models.Model):

    user = models.OneToOneField(settings.AUTH_USER_MODEL,
on_delete=models.CASCADE)

    bio = models.TextField(blank=True)

    location = models.CharField(max_length=100,
blank=True)

    profile_picture =
models.ImageField(upload_to='profile_pictures/',
blank=True)



    def __str__(self):

        return self.user.email
```

Signal to Create/Update User Profile

Use Django signals to automatically create or update the UserProfile when a CustomUser is created or updated. Add signals in library/signals.py:

```
from django.db.models.signals import post_save

from django.dispatch import receiver
```

```
from .models import CustomUser, UserProfile


@receiver(post_save, sender=CustomUser)
def create_user_profile(sender, instance, created,
**kwargs):
    if created:
        UserProfile.objects.create(user=instance)


@receiver(post_save, sender=CustomUser)
def save_user_profile(sender, instance, **kwargs):
    instance.userprofile.save()
```

Connect the signals in library/apps.py:

```
from django.apps import AppConfig


class LibraryConfig(AppConfig):
    name = 'library'


    def ready(self):
        import library.signals
```

Creating Forms for User Profile

UserProfile Form

Create a form to handle user profile updates. Add to library/forms.py:

```
from django import forms
from .models import UserProfile


class UserProfileForm(forms.ModelForm):
    class Meta:
        model = UserProfile
        fields = ['bio', 'location', 'profile_picture']
```

Creating Views and Templates

Views to Display and Edit Profiles

Add views to display and edit user profiles in library/views.py:

```
from django.shortcuts import render, redirect
from django.contrib.auth.decorators import login_required
from .forms import UserProfileForm
from .models import UserProfile


@login_required
def profile_view(request):
    profile = request.user.userprofile
    return render(request, 'library/profile.html',
{'profile': profile})
```

```
@login_required
def edit_profile_view(request):
    profile = request.user.userprofile
    if request.method == 'POST':
        form = UserProfileForm(request.POST,
request.FILES, instance=profile)
        if form.is_valid():
            form.save()
            return redirect('profile')
    else:
        form = UserProfileForm(instance=profile)
    return render(request, 'library/edit_profile.html',
{'form': form})
```

Templates for Displaying and Editing Profiles

Create library/templates/library/profile.html to display the user profile:

```
<!DOCTYPE html>
<html>
<head>
    <title>User Profile</title>
</head>
<body>
```

```
    <h2>User Profile</h2>

    <img src="{{ profile.profile_picture.url }}"
alt="Profile Picture">

    <p><strong>Email:</strong> {{ profile.user.email
}}</p>

    <p><strong>Bio:</strong> {{ profile.bio }}</p>

    <p><strong>Location:</strong> {{ profile.location
}}</p>

    <p><a href="{% url 'edit_profile' %}">Edit
Profile</a></p>

</body>

</html>
```

Create library/templates/library/edit_profile.html to edit the user profile:

```
<!DOCTYPE html>

<html>

<head>

    <title>Edit Profile</title>

</head>

<body>

    <h2>Edit Profile</h2>

    <form method="post" enctype="multipart/form-data">

        {% csrf_token %}
```

```
        {{ form.as_p }}

        <button type="submit">Save changes</button>

    </form>

</body>

</html>
```

Updating URLs

Add URLs for the profile views in library/urls.py:

```
from django.urls import path

from . import views


urlpatterns = [

    path('profile/', views.profile_view, name='profile'),

    path('profile/edit/', views.edit_profile_view,
name='edit_profile'),

]
```

Implementing Access Control

Create Groups and Permissions

Use the Django admin interface to create groups and assign permissions. For example, create a group called Editors with permissions to add and change books.

Use the @permission_required decorator to restrict access to views. Update library/views.py:

```
from django.contrib.auth.decorators import
permission_required
```

```
@permission_required('library.change_book',
raise_exception=True)
def edit_book_view(request, book_id):
    book = get_object_or_404(Book, id=book_id)
    if request.method == 'POST':
        form = BookForm(request.POST, instance=book)
        if form.is_valid():
            form.save()
            return redirect('book_list')
    else:
        form = BookForm(instance=book)
    return render(request, 'library/edit_book.html',
{'form': form})
```

This view ensures only users with the change_book permission can edit books.

Finally, navigate to http://127.0.0.1:8000/profile/ to view the user profile and http://127.0.0.1:8000/profile/edit/ to edit the user profile. Verify that only users with the appropriate permissions can access restricted views.

After completing these steps, you will have successfully set up the BookTech application's user profile and access control system. Making sure that only approved users can execute certain operations, managing user profiles, and implementing access control through permissions and groups are all part of this.

Summary

To summarize, we started by constructing a user registration form, handling user login and logout using Django's built-in views, and establishing the necessary URL patterns and templates. We then went over password management, including how to implement password change and reset functionality. This included customizing Django's built-in views for password change and reset, as well as generating the necessary templates to provide a pleasant user experience.

Then we looked into managing user rights and groups. We learnt how to apply particular permissions to users, check permissions in views with decorators and the has_perm method, and establish and manage groups using the Django admin interface. We also explored how to create new user models that augment the default user model. We explored the importance of custom user models in adding more features and functionalities, and we illustrated how to construct a custom user model, change settings, create user forms, and setup the Django admin to handle the custom user model.

The chapter ended with an interactive project in which we created a user profile and an access control mechanism. This included developing a user profile model, forms for profile modifications, views and templates for displaying and editing profiles, and implementing access control via rights and groups. Using these approaches, we ensured full user management and secure access control within the BookTech application.

Test Your Knowledge

1. What is the purpose of the AUTH_USER_MODEL setting in Django?

a) To specify the default model for storing session data
b) To define the model used for user authentication
c) To set the model used for permissions
d) To designate the model for logging user activities

Answer: b) To define the model used for user authentication

2. Which of the following is NOT a default permission provided by Django for models?

a) add
b) view
c) change
d) delete

Answer: b) view

3. What does the @permission_required decorator do in Django views?

a) Ensures a user is logged in before accessing the view
b) Checks if a user has a specific permission before accessing the view
c) Redirects users to the login page if they are not authenticated
d) Logs user activities when accessing the view

Answer: b) Checks if a user has a specific permission before accessing the view

4. Which method is used to create a superuser in a custom user model manager?

a) create_admin_user
b) create_superuser
c) create_staff_user
d) create_user

Answer: b) create_superuser

5. What field is used as the unique identifier for authentication in the custom user model provided in this chapter?

a) username
b) email
c) id
d) first_name

Answer: b) email

6. Which Django signal is used to automatically create or update a user profile when a user is created or updated?

a) pre_save
b) post_delete
c) post_save
d) pre_delete

Answer: c) post_save

7. How do you restrict access to a view to only logged-in users?

a) By using the @permission_required decorator
b) By checking the user's session data in the view
c) By using the @login_required decorator
d) By configuring URL patterns to allow only authenticated users

Answer: c) By using the @login_required decorator

8. Which template tag is used to render form fields in a Django template?

a) {{ form.fields }}
b) {% form.render %}
c) {{ form.as_p }}
d) {% form.fieldset %}

Answer: c) {{ form.as_p }}

9. What is the main advantage of using groups for managing permissions in Django?

a) It reduces the need for custom user models
b) It allows for easier management of permissions for multiple users

c) It automatically creates user profiles
d) It simplifies the database schema

Answer: b) It allows for easier management of permissions for multiple users

10. Which method in the custom user model manager ensures the email field is normalized before creating a user?

a) normalize_email
b) sanitize_email
c) validate_email
d) standardize_email

Answer: a) normalize_email

CHAPTER 7: ADVANCED DJANGO CAPABILITIES

Introduction

We have reached the point where we can start using Django's standard capabilities; now we will dive into its advanced capabilities, where we will explore strong features that improve the functionality and performance of your Django projects. This chapter begins with middleware, in which you will learn how to construct and use middleware to process requests and answers, hence increasing the flexibility and customization of your application. You'll look at signals, a strong mechanism for connecting distinct components in your program, and how components can communicate with one another without using direct references to improve modularity.

Another important subject that we will get into is caching, which helps applications run faster by keeping data that is accessed often in memory. You will learn how to use various caching algorithms to lower your application's load times and server demand. Asynchronous views are also learned to help you write views that can manage huge traffic efficiently. You will learn how to use Django's support for asynchronous programming to improve the responsiveness of your online apps. Then we will look at WebSockets to enable real-time communication, and we will learn how to use them to add features like real-time notifications to your application, making it more engaging and dynamic.

In the last section of the chapter, you'll find a hands-on exercise that allows you to integrate real-time notifications into the BookTech app. This hands-on exercise will combine the advanced ideas you've studied, guaranteeing that you can use these skills to build high-performance, responsive Django apps.

Middleware

What is Middleware?

Middleware in Django is a way to process requests and responses globally across your application. It's a layer that sits between the request and the view or between the view and the response, allowing you to process or modify these objects before they reach their destination. Middleware can be used for a variety of tasks such as logging, authentication, modifying headers, and handling errors.

Types of Middleware

Middleware can perform various functions in a Django application, including but not limited to:

- Security Middleware: Enhances security by managing headers, enforcing HTTPS, and preventing clickjacking.
- Session Middleware: Manages sessions across requests.
- Authentication Middleware: Associates users with requests using sessions.

- Message Middleware: Enables cookie- and session-based messaging.
- Compression Middleware: Compresses responses for faster delivery.
- Custom Middleware: Performs any custom tasks you need, such as logging, modifying request/response objects, or adding specific functionality.

Creating Custom Middleware in BookTech

We will create a custom middleware in our BookTech application that logs the duration of each request.

Define the Middleware Class

Create a file named middleware.py in your library application directory:

```
touch library/middleware.py
```

Open library/middleware.py and define the middleware class:

```
import time

import logging


logger = logging.getLogger(__name__)


class RequestLoggingMiddleware:

    def __init__(self, get_response):

        self.get_response = get_response


    def __call__(self, request):

        # Code to be executed for each request before

        # the view (and later middleware) are called.
```

```
        start_time = time.time()


        response = self.get_response(request)


        # Code to be executed for each request/response
after
        # the view is called.
        duration = time.time() - start_time
        logger.info(f"{request.method}
{request.get_full_path()} completed in {duration:.2f}s")


        return response
```

This middleware logs the time taken to process each request.

Add the Middleware to Settings

Open settings.py and add your custom middleware to the MIDDLEWARE setting:

```
MIDDLEWARE = [
    'django.middleware.security.SecurityMiddleware',

'django.contrib.sessions.middleware.SessionMiddleware',
    'django.middleware.common.CommonMiddleware',
    'django.middleware.csrf.CsrfViewMiddleware',
```

```
'django.contrib.auth.middleware.AuthenticationMiddleware'
,

'django.contrib.messages.middleware.MessageMiddleware',

'django.middleware.clickjacking.XFrameOptionsMiddleware',
    'library.middleware.RequestLoggingMiddleware',  # Add
this line
]
```

This ensures that Django processes the request through your custom middleware.

Configure Logging

Ensure logging is configured to output information to the console or a file. In settings.py, add or update the logging configuration:

```
LOGGING = {
    'version': 1,
    'disable_existing_loggers': False,
    'handlers': {
        'file': {
            'level': 'DEBUG',
            'class': 'logging.FileHandler',
            'filename': 'debug.log',
        },
```

```
        'console': {
            'level': 'DEBUG',
            'class': 'logging.StreamHandler',
        },
    },
    'loggers': {
        'django': {
            'handlers': ['console', 'file'],
            'level': 'DEBUG',
            'propagate': True,
        },
        'library': {
            'handlers': ['console', 'file'],
            'level': 'DEBUG',
            'propagate': True,
        },
    },
}
```

Open your browser and navigate through your application. You should see logs in your console or log file indicating the time taken to process each request.

Desired output:

```
[INFO] 127.0.0.1 GET /library/books/ completed in 0.02s
```

Middleware for Custom Functionality

Creating custom middleware can help you implement specific functionalities that need to be applied across your entire application. Following are a few more examples of what you can do with middleware:

- Block requests from specific IP addresses.
- Track user activities like page visits.
- Add custom headers to every response.
- Gracefully handle exceptions and log detailed error information.

To demonstrate another example, we will create middleware that adds a custom header to each response.

Define the Middleware Class

In library/middleware.py, add the following class:

```
class CustomHeaderMiddleware:
    def __init__(self, get_response):
        self.get_response = get_response

    def __call__(self, request):
        response = self.get_response(request)
        response['X-Custom-Header'] = 'BookTech'
        return response
```

Add the Middleware to Settings

In settings.py, add the CustomHeaderMiddleware to the MIDDLEWARE setting:

```
MIDDLEWARE = [
```

```
    'django.middleware.security.SecurityMiddleware',

'django.contrib.sessions.middleware.SessionMiddleware',
    'django.middleware.common.CommonMiddleware',
    'django.middleware.csrf.CsrfViewMiddleware',

'django.contrib.auth.middleware.AuthenticationMiddleware'
,

'django.contrib.messages.middleware.MessageMiddleware',

'django.middleware.clickjacking.XFrameOptionsMiddleware',
    'library.middleware.RequestLoggingMiddleware',
    'library.middleware.CustomHeaderMiddleware',  # Add
this line
]
```

Testing the Middleware

Restart the Django development server:

```
python manage.py runserver
```

Use a tool like curl or your browser's developer tools to inspect the response headers:

```
curl -I http://127.0.0.1:8000/library/books/
```

You should see the custom header in the response:

```
HTTP/1.1 200 OK
```

```
X-Custom-Header: BookTech
```

By following these steps, you have gained a good understanding of middleware and its various types. You have also built your own middleware to track how long requests take and to add your own custom headers.

Signals

Concept of Signal and Handler Mechanism

The signals provide a way to allow decoupled applications to get notified when certain events occur. They are useful for implementing a variety of behaviors without tightly coupling the code. Signals are dispatched when certain actions occur (like saving an object or a user logging in), and handlers (or receivers) are connected to these signals to perform specific actions in response.

Key Components of Django Signals

- Signal: The event or action that triggers the notification.
- Receiver (Handler): The function or method that receives the notification and performs an action.

Django provides several built-in signals, such as post_save, pre_save, post_delete, and pre_delete. You can also create your custom signals for more specific use cases.

Using Signals to Connect Components

We will practically implement signals in our BookTech application by connecting components for immediate responses to specific actions. We will connect a signal to a handler that sends a welcome email to new users upon registration.

Create the Signal Handler

First, create a signal handler function. Open library/signals.py and add the following:

```
from django.db.models.signals import post_save

from django.dispatch import receiver

from django.core.mail import send_mail

from .models import CustomUser
```

```
@receiver(post_save, sender=CustomUser)

def send_welcome_email(sender, instance, created,
**kwargs):

    if created:

        send_mail(

            'Welcome to BookTech',

            'Hi {},\n\nThank you for registering at
BookTech! We are excited to have you on
board.'.format(instance.first_name),

            'from@gitforgits.com',

            [instance.email],

            fail_silently=False,

        )
```

This handler listens for the post_save signal on the CustomUser model. When a new user is created, it sends a welcome email to the user's email address.

Connect Signal in the App Configuration

Ensure that the signals are connected when the application starts. Update library/apps.py:

```
from django.apps import AppConfig



class LibraryConfig(AppConfig):

    name = 'library'
```

```
    def ready(self):

        import library.signals
```

To verify the functionality, initiate the Django development server and navigate to http://127.0.0.1:8000/register/. Register a new user and check the email address provided during registration to see if the welcome email is received.

Custom Signals

In addition to built-in signals, you can create custom signals to respond to specific events in your application.

Create a Custom Signal

Define a custom signal in library/signals.py:

```
from django.dispatch import Signal



user_logged_in = Signal(providing_args=["user",
"timestamp"])
```

This custom signal is called user_logged_in and it provides user and timestamp arguments.

Send the Custom Signal

In your login view, send the custom signal when a user logs in. Update library/views.py:

```
from django.contrib.auth import authenticate, login

from django.shortcuts import render, redirect

from django.utils import timezone

from .signals import user_logged_in



def login_view(request):
```

```
    if request.method == 'POST':
        username = request.POST['username']
        password = request.POST['password']
        user = authenticate(request, username=username,
password=password)
        if user is not None:
            login(request, user)
            user_logged_in.send(sender=user.__class__,
user=user, timestamp=timezone.now())
            return redirect('book_list')
        else:
            return render(request,
'registration/login.html', {'error': 'Invalid
credentials'})
    return render(request, 'registration/login.html')
```

Handle the Custom Signal

Create a signal handler for the custom signal in library/signals.py:

```
from django.dispatch import receiver
from .signals import user_logged_in
import logging


logger = logging.getLogger(__name__)
```

```
@receiver(user_logged_in)
def log_user_login(sender, user, timestamp, **kwargs):
    logger.info(f"User {user.email} logged in at
{timestamp}")
```

This handler logs a message each time a user logs in.

Configure Logging

Ensure logging is configured in settings.py:

```
LOGGING = {
    'version': 1,
    'disable_existing_loggers': False,
    'handlers': {
        'file': {
            'level': 'DEBUG',
            'class': 'logging.FileHandler',
            'filename': 'debug.log',
        },
        'console': {
            'level': 'DEBUG',
            'class': 'logging.StreamHandler',
        },
```

```
    },
    'loggers': {
        'django': {
            'handlers': ['console', 'file'],
            'level': 'DEBUG',
            'propagate': True,
        },
        'library': {
            'handlers': ['console', 'file'],
            'level': 'DEBUG',
            'propagate': True,
        },
    },
}
```

To test the functionality, launch the Django development server and go to the specified URL in your browser. Log in with an existing user account and check the logs for the login message:

```
[INFO] User user@gitforgits.com logged in at 2024-06-15
12:34:56.789012
```

This approach of signal enhances the modularity and responsiveness of your Django applications.

Caching

Types of Caching

Caching is a technique used to store data temporarily to reduce the time needed to access it. It significantly improves the performance and scalability of web applications. Django supports various types of caching mechanisms:

1. Database Caching: Stores cache data in the database. It's simple to set up but can be slower than other methods.
2. File-Based Caching: Stores cache data in the filesystem. It's suitable for small to medium-sized applications but can be slower for large datasets.
3. In-Memory Caching: Uses memory-based stores like Memcached or Redis. It offers fast access and is ideal for high-performance applications.
4. Local Memory Caching: Stores cache data in the memory of the process handling the request. It's the fastest but only useful for single-process environments.
5. Custom Caching: Allows for custom cache backends to meet specific requirements.

Implementing Caching in BookTech

We will implement caching to improve the performance of our BookTech application by caching the list of books.

Setting up Caching in Django

First, choose the cache backend. For the below example, we will use file-based caching. Configure the cache in settings.py:

```
CACHES = {
    'default': {
        'BACKEND':
'django.core.cache.backends.filebased.FileBasedCache',
        'LOCATION': '/var/tmp/django_cache',
    }
}
```

Ensure the cache directory exists and has appropriate permissions:

```
mkdir -p /var/tmp/django_cache
```

Using Low-Level Cache API

Use Django's low-level cache API to cache data manually. Update the book_list view in library/views.py to cache the list of books:

```
from django.core.cache import cache

from django.shortcuts import render

from .models import Book


def book_list(request):

    # Check if the data is in the cache

    books = cache.get('all_books')

    if not books:

        # If not, fetch the data from the database and
store it in the cache

        books = Book.objects.all()

        cache.set('all_books', books, 300)  # Cache data
for 5 minutes (300 seconds)

    return render(request, 'library/book_list.html',
{'books': books})
```

This implementation checks if the list of books is in the cache. If not, it retrieves the data from the database and stores it in the cache for 5 minutes.

Template Fragment Caching

Use template fragment caching to cache specific parts of your templates. For example, cache the book list template fragment. Update library/templates/library/book_list.html:

```
{% load cache %}
```

```
{% cache 300 book_list %}

<ul>

    {% for book in books %}

        <li>{{ book.title }} by {{ book.author.first_name
}} {{ book.author.last_name }}</li>

    {% endfor %}

</ul>

{% endcache %}
```

This caches the book list HTML for 5 minutes.

View-Level Caching

Use Django's view-level caching to cache the entire view output. Update library/urls.py to cache the book_list view:

```
from django.urls import path

from django.views.decorators.cache import cache_page

from . import views


urlpatterns = [

    path('books/', cache_page(300)(views.book_list),
name='book_list'),

]
```

This caches the book_list view output for 5 minutes.

To test the functionality, launch the Django development server and go to the specified URL in your browser. The first request fetches the data from the database and caches it. Subsequent requests within 5 minutes will serve the cached data.

Using Memcached for In-Memory Caching

For improved performance, switch to an in-memory cache like Memcached. First, install Memcached and the Python binding:

```
sudo apt-get install memcached

pip install python-memcached
```

Update the cache configuration in settings.py:

```
CACHES = {

    'default': {

        'BACKEND':
'django.core.cache.backends.memcached.MemcachedCache',

        'LOCATION': '127.0.0.1:11211',

    }

}
```

With this configuration, the cache data is stored in Memcached, offering faster access compared to file-based caching.

Advanced Cache Usage

Implement more advanced caching techniques such as per-site caching or caching specific data models. For example, use the cache_page decorator to cache different views for different durations.

```
from django.views.decorators.cache import cache_page



urlpatterns = [
```

```
    path('books/', cache_page(300)(views.book_list),
name='book_list'),

    path('book/<int:id>/',
cache_page(600)(views.book_detail), name='book_detail'),

]
```

This will store the book detail view in a cache for 10 minutes and the book list view for 500 milliseconds. With caching, your Django app will run much faster by decreasing database load and increasing response times.

Asynchronous Views

Benefits of Asynchronous Views

Asynchronous views in Django allow you to handle a large number of requests concurrently, improving the overall performance and responsiveness of your application. Traditional synchronous views block the execution of other requests until they complete, which can lead to inefficiencies, especially when dealing with I/O-bound tasks like network calls or database queries. Asynchronous views, on the other hand, do not block other operations, allowing for more efficient handling of tasks and better resource utilization.

Key benefits include:

- Handle more requests simultaneously, reducing wait times and increasing throughput.
- Efficiently manage tasks that involve I/O operations, such as database access or API calls.
- Better scalability for applications with high traffic or resource-intensive operations.

Writing Asynchronous Views

We will implement an asynchronous view in our BookTech application. We will create an asynchronous view that fetches book data and simulates a network delay to demonstrate the benefits.

Ensure Django is set up to handle asynchronous views by verifying your ASGI configuration in asgi.py. Typically, this file is already configured correctly if you started with a recent version of Django.

Creating the Asynchronous View

Update library/views.py to include an asynchronous view for fetching book data:

```
import asyncio
from django.http import JsonResponse
from django.shortcuts import get_object_or_404
from .models import Book


async def async_book_list(request):
    await asyncio.sleep(2)  # Simulate a network delay
    books = await Book.objects.all().values('title',
'author__first_name', 'author__last_name')
    return JsonResponse(list(books), safe=False)


async def async_book_detail(request, book_id):
    await asyncio.sleep(2)  # Simulate a network delay
    book = await get_object_or_404(Book, id=book_id)
    data = {
        'title': book.title,
        'author': f"{book.author.first_name}
{book.author.last_name}",
        'publication_date': book.publication_date,
        'isbn': book.isbn,
    }
```

```
    return JsonResponse(data)
```

These asynchronous views simulate a delay to demonstrate the non-blocking nature of asynchronous operations.

Updating URLs

Add URL patterns for the asynchronous views in library/urls.py:

```
from django.urls import path

from . import views


urlpatterns = [

    path('async/books/', views.async_book_list,
name='async_book_list'),

    path('async/book/<int:book_id>/',
views.async_book_detail, name='async_book_detail'),

]
```

Testing the Asynchronous Views

Start the Django development server:

```
python manage.py runserver
```

Open your browser or use a tool like curl to test the asynchronous endpoints:

```
curl http://127.0.0.1:8000/async/books/

curl http://127.0.0.1:8000/async/book/1/
```

You should see the list of books and the details of a specific book in JSON format, with a simulated delay.

Demonstrating Improved Performance

To demonstrate the improved performance, we will compare the handling of multiple requests with synchronous and asynchronous views.

- Synchronous View for Comparison

Add a synchronous view to simulate a delay in library/views.py:

```
from time import sleep


def sync_book_list(request):
    sleep(2)  # Simulate a network delay
    books = Book.objects.all().values('title',
'author__first_name', 'author__last_name')
    return JsonResponse(list(books), safe=False)


def sync_book_detail(request, book_id):
    sleep(2)  # Simulate a network delay
    book = get_object_or_404(Book, id=book_id)
    data = {
        'title': book.title,
        'author': f"{book.author.first_name}
{book.author.last_name}",
        'publication_date': book.publication_date,
        'isbn': book.isbn,
    }
```

```
    return JsonResponse(data)
```

Add URL patterns for the synchronous views in library/urls.py:

```
urlpatterns += [
    path('sync/books/', views.sync_book_list,
name='sync_book_list'),
    path('sync/book/<int:book_id>/',
views.sync_book_detail, name='sync_book_detail'),
]
```

- Benchmarking

Use a tool like ab (ApacheBench) to benchmark the performance of the synchronous and asynchronous views.

```
ab -n 10 -c 2 http://127.0.0.1:8000/sync/books/
ab -n 10 -c 2 http://127.0.0.1:8000/async/books/
```

The asynchronous views should handle the concurrent requests more efficiently, showing lower response times and higher throughput compared to the synchronous views.

By implementing asynchronous views in BookTech, you are able to handle high-traffic scenarios more efficiently, improving the responsiveness and scalability of your application, especially for I/O-bound tasks.

WebSockets with Channels

Overview

WebSockets enable real-time, two-way communication between clients and servers, which is essential for features like live notifications, chat applications, and real-time updates. Django Channels extend Django to handle WebSockets and other asynchronous protocols. This allows Django to support real-time communication, making your application more dynamic and interactive.

Setting up Django Channels

Install Django Channels

First, install Django Channels and its dependencies:

```
pip install channels
```

Update Settings

Update settings.py to configure Channels. Add channels to your INSTALLED_APPS and define the ASGI_APPLICATION:

```
INSTALLED_APPS = [
    'django.contrib.admin',
    'django.contrib.auth',
    'django.contrib.contenttypes',
    'django.contrib.sessions',
    'django.contrib.messages',
    'django.contrib.staticfiles',
    'channels',
    'library',  # Your app
]


ASGI_APPLICATION = 'BookTech.asgi.application'
```

Create asgi.py

Create an asgi.py file at the root of your project (next to settings.py):

```
import os
from channels.routing import ProtocolTypeRouter,
URLRouter
from channels.auth import AuthMiddlewareStack
from django.core.asgi import get_asgi_application
from library import routing


os.environ.setdefault('DJANGO_SETTINGS_MODULE',
'BookTech.settings')


application = ProtocolTypeRouter({
    "http": get_asgi_application(),
    "websocket": AuthMiddlewareStack(
        URLRouter(
            routing.websocket_urlpatterns
        )
    ),
})
```

Create Routing for Channels

Create a routing.py file in your library app:

```
from django.urls import path
from . import consumers
```

```
websocket_urlpatterns = [

    path('ws/notifications/',
consumers.NotificationConsumer.as_asgi()),

]
```

Create a Consumer

Consumers handle WebSocket connections. Create a consumers.py file in your library app:

```
import json

from channels.generic.websocket import
AsyncWebsocketConsumer


class NotificationConsumer(AsyncWebsocketConsumer):

    async def connect(self):

        await self.accept()


    async def disconnect(self, close_code):

        pass


    async def receive(self, text_data):

        data = json.loads(text_data)

        message = data['message']
```

```
        # Echo the message back to the client
        await self.send(text_data=json.dumps({
            'message': message
        }))
```

Configure Channels Layer

To enable the channel layer for real-time communication, install Redis:

```
sudo apt-get install redis-server
pip install channels_redis
```

Update settings.py to use Redis as the channel layer backend:

```
CHANNEL_LAYERS = {
    'default': {
        'BACKEND':
'channels_redis.core.RedisChannelLayer',
        'CONFIG': {
            "hosts": [('127.0.0.1', 6379)],
        },
    },
}
```

Implementing Real-Time Notifications

Create a Notification System

Update the NotificationConsumer to handle sending notifications. Modify consumers.py:

```
import json
from channels.generic.websocket import
AsyncWebsocketConsumer


class NotificationConsumer(AsyncWebsocketConsumer):
    async def connect(self):
        self.group_name = 'notifications'
        await self.channel_layer.group_add(
            self.group_name,
            self.channel_name
        )
        await self.accept()

    async def disconnect(self, close_code):
        await self.channel_layer.group_discard(
            self.group_name,
            self.channel_name
        )

    async def receive(self, text_data):
        data = json.loads(text_data)
        message = data['message']
```

```
        # Broadcast message to group
        await self.channel_layer.group_send(
            self.group_name,
            {
                'type': 'send_notification',
                'message': message
            }
        )

    async def send_notification(self, event):
        message = event['message']

        # Send message to WebSocket
        await self.send(text_data=json.dumps({
            'message': message
        }))
```

Creating Frontend WebSocket Integration

Update your HTML template to include JavaScript for handling WebSocket connections. Create library/templates/library/notifications.html:

```
<!DOCTYPE html>
```

```
<html>
<head>
    <title>Real-Time Notifications</title>
</head>
<body>
    <h1>Real-Time Notifications</h1>
    <ul id="notifications"></ul>
    <script>
        const notifications =
document.getElementById('notifications');
        const socket = new WebSocket('ws://' +
window.location.host + '/ws/notifications/');

        socket.onmessage = function(event) {
            const data = JSON.parse(event.data);
            const message = data.message;
            const li = document.createElement('li');
            li.textContent = message;
            notifications.appendChild(li);
        };

        function sendNotification() {
```

```
            const message = "New notification at " + new
Date().toLocaleTimeString();
            socket.send(JSON.stringify({'message':
message}));
        }

        setInterval(sendNotification, 5000);  // Send a
notification every 5 seconds
    </script>
</body>
</html>
```

Update URL Patterns

Add a URL pattern for the notifications page in library/urls.py:

```
from django.urls import path
from . import views

urlpatterns = [
    path('notifications/', views.notifications_view,
name='notifications'),
]
```

And create the view in library/views.py:

```
from django.shortcuts import render
```

```
def notifications_view(request):

    return render(request, 'library/notifications.html')
```

To verify the functionality, initiate the Django development server and navigate to http://127.0.0.1:8000/notifications/. You should see real-time notifications appearing every 5 seconds, demonstrating WebSocket communication with Django Channels.

This above practical implementation shows how to set up WebSocket connections, create consumers, and handle real-time data in your BookTech application successfully.

Hands-on Lab: Adding Real-Time Notification

In this hands-on practice, we will add real-time notifications to the BookTech application using Django Channels and WebSockets. This feature will allow users to receive instant updates when certain events occur, such as a new book being added to the catalog.

Create the Notification Model

First, create a Notification model to store notifications. Update library/models.py:

```
from django.db import models

from django.conf import settings



class Notification(models.Model):

    user = models.ForeignKey(settings.AUTH_USER_MODEL,
on_delete=models.CASCADE)

    message = models.TextField()

    created_at = models.DateTimeField(auto_now_add=True)

    read = models.BooleanField(default=False)
```

```
    def __str__(self):
        return f'Notification for {self.user} at
{self.created_at}'
```

Create a Consumer for WebSocket Communication

Update library/consumers.py to handle WebSocket connections for notifications:

```
import json
from channels.generic.websocket import
AsyncWebsocketConsumer


class NotificationConsumer(AsyncWebsocketConsumer):
    async def connect(self):
        self.user = self.scope['user']
        if not self.user.is_authenticated:
            await self.close()
        else:
            self.group_name =
f'notifications_{self.user.id}'
            await self.channel_layer.group_add(
                self.group_name,
                self.channel_name
            )
            await self.accept()
```

```
async def disconnect(self, close_code):
    await self.channel_layer.group_discard(
        self.group_name,
        self.channel_name
    )

async def receive(self, text_data):
    data = json.loads(text_data)
    message = data['message']
    await self.channel_layer.group_send(
        self.group_name,
        {
            'type': 'send_notification',
            'message': message
        }
    )

async def send_notification(self, event):
    message = event['message']
    await self.send(text_data=json.dumps({
```

```
            'message': message
        }))
```

Create Routing for WebSockets

Ensure your library/routing.py is set up for the new consumer:

```
from django.urls import path
from . import consumers


websocket_urlpatterns = [
    path('ws/notifications/',
consumers.NotificationConsumer.as_asgi()),
]
```

Update Views to Trigger Notifications

Modify the add_book_view to send a notification when a new book is added. Update library/views.py:

```
from django.shortcuts import render, redirect
from django.contrib.auth.decorators import login_required
from django.core.cache import cache
from .models import Book, Notification
from .forms import BookForm
from channels.layers import get_channel_layer
from asgiref.sync import async_to_sync
import json
```

```
@login_required
def add_book_view(request):
    if request.method == 'POST':
        form = BookForm(request.POST)
        if form.is_valid():
            book = form.save()
            # Invalidate cache
            cache.delete('all_books')
            # Create a notification for all users
            users = User.objects.all()
            for user in users:
                Notification.objects.create(user=user,
message=f'New book added: {book.title}')
                # Send real-time notification
                channel_layer = get_channel_layer()
                async_to_sync(channel_layer.group_send)(
                    f'notifications_{user.id}',
                    {
                        'type': 'send_notification',
                        'message': f'New book added:
{book.title}'
```

```
                    }

                )

            return redirect('book_list')

    else:

        form = BookForm()

    return render(request, 'library/add_book.html',
{'form': form})
```

Create Templates for Real-Time Notifications

Add a new template to display notifications. Create library/templates/library/notifications.html:

```
<!DOCTYPE html>

<html>

<head>

    <title>Real-Time Notifications</title>

</head>

<body>

    <h1>Real-Time Notifications</h1>

    <ul id="notifications"></ul>

    <script>

        const notifications =
document.getElementById('notifications');

        const socket = new WebSocket('ws://' +
window.location.host + '/ws/notifications/');
```

```
        socket.onmessage = function(event) {
            const data = JSON.parse(event.data);
            const message = data.message;
            const li = document.createElement('li');
            li.textContent = message;
            notifications.appendChild(li);
        };
    </script>
</body>
</html>
```

Update URL Patterns

Add a URL pattern for the notifications page in library/urls.py:

```
from django.urls import path
from . import views


urlpatterns = [
    path('notifications/', views.notifications_view,
name='notifications'),
]
```

Create the view in library/views.py:

```
from django.shortcuts import render


def notifications_view(request):

    return render(request, 'library/notifications.html')
```

Open two browser windows: one for adding a book (http://127.0.0.1:8000/library/add/) and another for viewing notifications (http://127.0.0.1:8000/notifications/). When you add a new book, you should see the notification appear in real-time on the notifications page.

Summary

This chapter focused on learning Django's enhanced capabilities to improve web application efficiency and interaction. Middleware was created as a powerful tool for processing requests and responses on a global scale, enabling activities like logging, authentication, and custom header management. We introduced the idea of signals and showed how they work by sending a welcome email to new users when they join up, illustrating how decoupled applications can communicate with each other through the notification of unique occurrences.

Caching methods were learned to increase application performance by lowering load times and server demand. To improve data retrieval, various caching techniques were used, including file-based and in-memory caching with Memcached. Asynchronous views were implemented to process several requests concurrently, improving the application's efficiency and responsiveness, especially for I/O-bound operations. The chapter taught WebSockets and Django Channels, demonstrating how they enable real-time, two-way communication between clients and servers. A practical implementation of real-time notifications was demonstrated, including how to integrate WebSockets into the BookTech application. This included configuring Django Channels, developing a consumer for managing WebSocket connections, and changing views to send notifications when specified actions occurred, such as adding a new book.

Finally, a hands-on program of real-time notifications in the BookTech application was demonstrated. This hands-on project highlighted the practical implementation of previously acquired topics, such as configuring WebSocket routing, producing and handling notifications in the frontend, and assuring real-time updates for users. This chapter taught you how to create advanced features that improve the performance and user experience of your Django apps.

Test Your Knowledge

1. What is the primary purpose of middleware in Django?

a) To handle user authentication
b) To process requests and responses globally
c) To manage database connections
d) To render templates

Answer: b) To process requests and responses globally

2. Which method is used to connect a signal to a handler in Django?

a) connect_signal
b) attach_signal
c) bind_signal
d) @receiver

Answer: d) @receiver

3. What caching backend would you use for high-performance, in-memory caching in Django?

a) File-based caching
b) Database caching
c) Memcached
d) Local memory caching

Answer: c) Memcached

4. What is the main advantage of using asynchronous views in Django?

a) Simplifies database queries
b) Enhances template rendering
c) Handles high-traffic efficiently with non-blocking I/O
d) Provides built-in security features

Answer: c) Handles high-traffic efficiently with non-blocking I/O

5. Which file in a Django project is typically modified to configure Channels and WebSockets?

a) settings.py
b) urls.py
c) views.py
d) asgi.py

Answer: d) asgi.py

6. Which Channels component is responsible for handling WebSocket connections in Django?

a) Middleware
b) Consumer

c) Signal
d) Template

Answer: b) Consumer

7. What function is used to send data over a WebSocket connection in Django Channels?

a) send_data
b) send_json
c) send
d) send_message

Answer: c) send

8. How do you ensure a user is authenticated before they can connect to a WebSocket in Django Channels?

a) By adding a login check in the view
b) By using AuthMiddlewareStack in the ASGI application
c) By modifying the settings.py file
d) By implementing a custom authentication backend

Answer: b) By using AuthMiddlewareStack in the ASGI application

9. Which Django feature allows for real-time notifications by leveraging WebSockets?

a) Middleware
b) Caching
c) Channels
d) Signals

Answer: c) Channels

10. What is the correct way to add a new WebSocket URL pattern for notifications in Django Channels?

a) path('notifications/', views.notifications_view)
b) path('ws/notifications/', consumers.NotificationConsumer.as_asgi())
c) url('notifications/', consumers.NotificationConsumer)
d) url('ws/notifications/', views.notifications_view)

Answer: b) path('ws/notifications/', consumers.NotificationConsumer.as_asgi())

CHAPTER 8: WORKING WITH MONGODB

Introduction

In this chapter, we will learn how to combine MongoDB with Django to improve the BookTech application. To begin, we will introduce NoSQL databases and explore the advantages of utilizing MongoDB, which is known for its flexibility, scalability, and ease of use. We next tell you how to set up MongoDB and configure it such that it works flawlessly with Django. This includes installing the necessary tools and libraries, as well as configuring Django's settings to connect to MongoDB.

Next, we will look at CRUD operations, which will teach you how to use Django to create, read, update, and remove documents in MongoDB. You will be able to better manage your data with these realistic methods. Then, we will look at MongoDB's sophisticated querying features, and you'll learn how to use the powerful query language to do complex searches and data retrievals. In addition, we will go over indexing and aggregation to improve data retrieval and data aggregation to gain insights from your data.

To wrap things off, we will have you implement MongoDB for the BookTech catalog. This hands-on project will combine all of the principles and abilities you've studied in this chapter, allowing you to test the power and flexibility of MongoDB within your Django application.

Setting up MongoDB

Benefits of NoSQL Databases

NoSQL databases offer several advantages over traditional relational databases, making them particularly well-suited for modern web applications. Key benefits include:

- Flexibility: NoSQL databases allow for dynamic schema design. You can easily add or remove fields, which is beneficial for applications with evolving data requirements.
- Scalability: They are designed to scale out by distributing data across multiple servers. This horizontal scalability is crucial for handling large volumes of traffic and data.
- Performance: NoSQL databases are optimized for high performance, especially for read and write operations. They can handle large amounts of data and high transaction rates.
- Complex Data Types: They support a variety of data types, including JSON-like documents, which align well with the data structures used in web applications.
- Ease of Use: NoSQL databases often provide simple APIs for CRUD operations, making them easier to work with compared to SQL.

Introduction to MongoDB

MongoDB is a popular NoSQL database that stores data in a flexible, JSON-like format called

BSON (Binary JSON). It is designed to handle large volumes of data and provide high availability and scalability. MongoDB's document-oriented structure allows for nested documents and arrays, making it easy to represent complex data relationships.

Setting up MongoDB

Installing MongoDB

To get started with MongoDB, install it on your system. Follow the installation instructions based on your operating system as below:

```
sudo apt update

sudo apt install -y mongodb
```

Start the MongoDB service:

```
sudo systemctl start mongodb

sudo systemctl enable mongodb
```

Verify the installation:

```
mongo --version
```

Configuring MongoDB with Django

To integrate MongoDB with Django, we will use the djongo library, which allows Django to communicate with MongoDB using Django's ORM.

Install djongo and pymongo:

```
pip install djongo pymongo
```

Updating Django Settings

Configure Django to use MongoDB as the database backend. Update settings.py:

```
DATABASES = {

    'default': {
```

```
        'ENGINE': 'djongo',
        'NAME': 'booktech_db',
    }
}
```

This configuration tells Django to use the djongo engine to connect to a MongoDB database named booktech_db.

Creating Models

Define your Django models as usual. Djongo will handle the translation of these models into MongoDB collections. For example, update library/models.py to include a model for books:

```
from django.db import models


class Author(models.Model):
    first_name = models.CharField(max_length=50)
    last_name = models.CharField(max_length=50)
    birth_date = models.DateField()

    def __str__(self):
        return f"{self.first_name} {self.last_name}"


class Book(models.Model):
    title = models.CharField(max_length=200)
```

```
    author = models.ForeignKey(Author,
on_delete=models.CASCADE)

    publication_date = models.DateField()

    isbn = models.CharField(max_length=13)

    summary = models.TextField()


    def __str__(self):

        return self.title
```

Running Migrations

Run Django's migration commands to create the necessary collections in MongoDB:

```
python manage.py makemigrations

python manage.py migrate
```

Connecting to MongoDB Shell

You can interact with MongoDB directly using the MongoDB shell. This allows you to inspect your collections and documents:

```
mongo
```

Switch to the booktech_db database:

```
use booktech_db
```

List collections:

```
show collections
```

Query documents:

```
db.book.find()
```

Sample Program: Up and Running with MongoDB

Creating Sample Data

We will add some sample data to our BookTech application. Use Django's admin interface or create a management command to populate the database. For simplicity, we will add data directly using Django's shell:

```
python manage.py shell
```

Inside the shell, create some authors and books:

```
from library.models import Author, Book



author1 = Author.objects.create(first_name='John',
last_name='Doe', birth_date='1980-01-01')

author2 = Author.objects.create(first_name='Jane',
last_name='Smith', birth_date='1975-05-15')



Book.objects.create(title='Book One', author=author1,
publication_date='2023-01-01', isbn='1234567890123',
summary='A fascinating book one.')

Book.objects.create(title='Book Two', author=author2,
publication_date='2023-02-01', isbn='9876543210987',
summary='A fascinating book two.')
```

Querying Data

Use Django's ORM to query data from MongoDB. Update library/views.py to display the list of books:

```python
from django.shortcuts import render

from .models import Book


def book_list(request):

    books = Book.objects.all()

    return render(request, 'library/book_list.html',
{'books': books})
```

Create a template to display the books in library/templates/library/book_list.html:

```html
<!DOCTYPE html>

<html>

<head>

    <title>Book List</title>

</head>

<body>

    <h1>Book List</h1>

    <ul>

        {% for book in books %}

            <li>{{ book.title }} by {{
book.author.first_name }} {{ book.author.last_name
}}</li>

        {% endfor %}

    </ul>
```

```
</body>

</html>
```

To verify the functionality, initiate the Django development server and navigate to http://127.0.0.1:8000/library/books/. You should see the list of books fetched from MongoDB.

CRUD Operations

In this section, we will demonstrate how to perform CRUD operations in the BookTech application using MongoDB. We will utilize Django's ORM, which works seamlessly with MongoDB through the djongo library.

Creating Documents

Creating documents in MongoDB using Django's ORM is similar to working with a relational database.

In library/views.py, add a view to handle book creation:

```
from django.shortcuts import render, redirect

from .forms import BookForm


def add_book_view(request):

    if request.method == 'POST':

        form = BookForm(request.POST)

        if form.is_valid():

            form.save()

            return redirect('book_list')

    else:

        form = BookForm()
```

```
    return render(request, 'library/add_book.html',
{'form': form})
```

Ensure you have a form for Book in library/forms.py:

```
from django import forms

from .models import Book


class BookForm(forms.ModelForm):

    class Meta:

        model = Book

        fields = ['title', 'author', 'publication_date',
'isbn', 'summary']
```

Create the template library/templates/library/add_book.html:

```
<!DOCTYPE html>

<html>

<head>

    <title>Add Book</title>

</head>

<body>

    <h1>Add a New Book</h1>

    <form method="post">

        {% csrf_token %}
```

```
        {{ form.as_p }}
        <button type="submit">Add Book</button>
    </form>
</body>
</html>
```

Add a URL pattern for this view in library/urls.py:

```
from django.urls import path
from . import views


urlpatterns = [
    path('books/add/', views.add_book_view,
name='add_book'),
]
```

To verify the functionality, initiate the Django development server and navigate to http://127.0.0.1:8000/books/add/. Fill in the form to add a new book, and it will be saved in MongoDB.

Reading Documents

Reading documents from MongoDB is straightforward with Django's ORM.

Update library/views.py to include a view that lists all books:

```
def book_list_view(request):
    books = Book.objects.all()
```

```
    return render(request, 'library/book_list.html',
{'books': books})
```

Ensure the template library/templates/library/book_list.html is set up to display the books:

```
<!DOCTYPE html>

<html>

<head>

    <title>Book List</title>

</head>

<body>

    <h1>Book List</h1>

    <ul>

        {% for book in books %}

            <li>{{ book.title }} by {{
book.author.first_name }} {{ book.author.last_name
}}</li>

        {% endfor %}

    </ul>

</body>

</html>
```

Add a URL pattern for this view in library/urls.py:

```
urlpatterns += [
```

```
    path('books/', views.book_list_view,
name='book_list'),

]
```

Navigate to http://127.0.0.1:8000/books/ to see the list of books retrieved from MongoDB.

Updating Documents

Updating documents involves fetching the document, populating a form with its data, and saving the updated data.

In library/views.py, add a view to handle book editing:

```
from django.shortcuts import get_object_or_404


def edit_book_view(request, book_id):

    book = get_object_or_404(Book, id=book_id)

    if request.method == 'POST':

        form = BookForm(request.POST, instance=book)

        if form.is_valid():

            form.save()

            return redirect('book_list')

    else:

        form = BookForm(instance=book)

    return render(request, 'library/edit_book.html',
{'form': form, 'book_id': book_id})
```

Create the template library/templates/library/edit_book.html:

```
<!DOCTYPE html>

<html>

<head>

    <title>Edit Book</title>

</head>

<body>

    <h1>Edit Book</h1>

    <form method="post">

        {% csrf_token %}

        {{ form.as_p }}

        <button type="submit">Save Changes</button>

    </form>

</body>

</html>
```

Add a URL pattern for this view in library/urls.py:

```
urlpatterns += [

    path('books/edit/<int:book_id>/',
views.edit_book_view, name='edit_book'),

]
```

Navigate to http://127.0.0.1:8000/books/. Click on a book to edit (ensure your book list template includes edit links), make changes, and save them. The changes will be updated in MongoDB.

Deleting Documents

Deleting documents involves confirming the deletion and then removing the document from the database.

In library/views.py, add a view to handle book deletion:

```
def delete_book_view(request, book_id):

    book = get_object_or_404(Book, id=book_id)

    if request.method == 'POST':

        book.delete()

        return redirect('book_list')

    return render(request, 'library/delete_book.html',
{'book': book})
```

Create the template library/templates/library/delete_book.html:

```
<!DOCTYPE html>

<html>

<head>

    <title>Delete Book</title>

</head>

<body>

    <h1>Delete Book</h1>

    <p>Are you sure you want to delete "{{ book.title
}}"?</p>

    <form method="post">

        {% csrf_token %}
```

```
        <button type="submit">Yes, delete</button>
    </form>
    <a href="{% url 'book_list' %}">Cancel</a>
</body>
</html>
```

Add a URL pattern for this view in library/urls.py:

```
urlpatterns += [
    path('books/delete/<int:book_id>/',
views.delete_book_view, name='delete_book'),
]
```

Navigate to http://127.0.0.1:8000/books/. Click on a book to delete, confirm deletion, and the book will be removed from MongoDB. By following the above steps, you can perform CRUD operations on documents in the BookTech application.

Advanced Queries

In this section, we will explore how to utilize MongoDB's powerful query language to perform advanced queries on the BookTech application's database. We will cover queries such as filtering, sorting, and aggregating data, leveraging MongoDB's capabilities to extract meaningful information efficiently.

Setting up Advanced Queries

Basic Filtering

MongoDB allows you to filter documents based on specific criteria. In Django, you can use the ORM's filtering methods to perform these operations.

For example, find all books published after a certain date:

```
from django.shortcuts import render
```

```
from .models import Book


def recent_books_view(request):
    recent_books =
Book.objects.filter(publication_date__gt='2023-01-01')
    return render(request, 'library/recent_books.html',
{'books': recent_books})
```

Create a template library/templates/library/recent_books.html:

```
<!DOCTYPE html>
<html>
<head>
    <title>Recent Books</title>
</head>
<body>
    <h1>Books Published After January 1, 2023</h1>
    <ul>
        {% for book in books %}
            <li>{{ book.title }} by {{
book.author.first_name }} {{ book.author.last_name
}}</li>
        {% endfor %}
    </ul>
```

```
</body>

</html>
```

Add a URL pattern for this view in library/urls.py:

```
urlpatterns += [

    path('books/recent/', views.recent_books_view,
name='recent_books'),

]
```

Complex Filtering

You can perform complex filtering using logical operators. For example, find all books by a specific author and published within a date range. For example, find books by 'John Doe' published between 2022 and 2023:

```
from django.shortcuts import render

from .models import Book, Author



def author_books_view(request):

    author = Author.objects.get(first_name='John',
last_name='Doe')

    author_books = Book.objects.filter(author=author,
publication_date__range=['2022-01-01', '2023-12-31'])

    return render(request, 'library/author_books.html',
{'books': author_books})
```

Create a template library/templates/library/author_books.html:

```
<!DOCTYPE html>
```

```
<html>

<head>

    <title>Books by John Doe</title>

</head>

<body>

    <h1>Books by John Doe Published Between 2022 and
2023</h1>

    <ul>

        {% for book in books %}

            <li>{{ book.title }}</li>

        {% endfor %}

    </ul>

</body>

</html>
```

Add a URL pattern for this view in library/urls.py:

```
urlpatterns += [

    path('books/author/', views.author_books_view,
name='author_books'),

]
```

Sorting Results

MongoDB supports sorting query results. In Django, you can use the order_by method to sort querysets. For example, list all books sorted by publication date in descending order:

```
def sorted_books_view(request):

    sorted_books = Book.objects.all().order_by('-
publication_date')

    return render(request, 'library/sorted_books.html',
{'books': sorted_books})
```

Create a template library/templates/library/sorted_books.html:

```
<!DOCTYPE html>

<html>

<head>

    <title>Books Sorted by Publication Date</title>

</head>

<body>

    <h1>Books Sorted by Publication Date (Newest
First)</h1>

    <ul>

        {% for book in books %}

                <li>{{ book.title }} - Published on {{
book.publication_date }}</li>

        {% endfor %}

    </ul>

</body>

</html>
```

Add a URL pattern for this view in library/urls.py:

```
urlpatterns += [

    path('books/sorted/', views.sorted_books_view,
name='sorted_books'),

]
```

Using Aggregation

Aggregation operations process data records and return computed results. MongoDB's aggregation framework is particularly powerful for generating complex reports and analytics. For example, count the number of books published each year:

```
from djongo.models import Count

from django.shortcuts import render



def books_per_year_view(request):

    books_per_year =
Book.objects.values('publication_date__year').annotate(co
unt=Count('id')).order_by('publication_date__year')

    return render(request, 'library/books_per_year.html',
{'data': books_per_year})
```

Create a template library/templates/library/books_per_year.html:

```
<!DOCTYPE html>

<html>

<head>

    <title>Books Per Year</title>
```

```
</head>

<body>

    <h1>Number of Books Published Each Year</h1>

    <ul>

        {% for entry in data %}

            <li>{{ entry.publication_date__year }}: {{ entry.count }} books</li>

        {% endfor %}

    </ul>

</body>

</html>
```

Add a URL pattern for this view in library/urls.py:

```
urlpatterns += [

    path('books/per_year/', views.books_per_year_view, name='books_per_year'),

]
```

Text Search

MongoDB supports text search indexes for searching within string fields. For example, perform a text search for books containing a specific keyword in the title or summary as below:

- Ensure your Book model includes text fields:

```
from djongo import models

from django.utils.text import slugify
```

```
class Book(models.Model):

    title = models.CharField(max_length=200)

    author = models.ForeignKey(Author,
on_delete=models.CASCADE)

    publication_date = models.DateField()

    isbn = models.CharField(max_length=13)

    summary = models.TextField()


    class Meta:

        indexes = [

            models.Index(fields=['title', 'summary']),

        ]
```

- Create a view to perform text search:

```
from django.db.models import Q


def search_books_view(request):

    query = request.GET.get('q')

    if query:

        results =
Book.objects.filter(Q(title__icontains=query) |
Q(summary__icontains=query))
```

```
    else:
        results = Book.objects.none()
    return render(request, 'library/search_results.html',
{'results': results})
```

- Create a template library/templates/library/search_results.html:

```
<!DOCTYPE html>
<html>
<head>
    <title>Search Results</title>
</head>
<body>
    <h1>Search Results</h1>
    <ul>
        {% for book in results %}
            <li>{{ book.title }} - {{ book.summary
}}</li>
        {% endfor %}
    </ul>
    <a href="{% url 'book_list' %}">Back to Book List</a>
</body>
</html>
```

- Add a URL pattern for this view in library/urls.py:

```
urlpatterns += [

    path('books/search/', views.search_books_view,
name='search_books'),

]
```

Go ahead and test out all those advanced queries by visiting their respective URLs. The aggregated, sorted, and filtered data should appear as anticipated.

Summary

So, to summarize, we focused on connecting MongoDB, a NoSQL database, with the BookTech application and executing CRUD operations. The chapter began with presenting NoSQL databases and stressing their advantages, such as flexibility, scalability, and performance. The setup process involved installing MongoDB, setting Django to connect to MongoDB via the djongo module, and creating Django models that translate to MongoDB collections. The chapter then showed how to do CRUD tasks. A form was set up to add new books, which were subsequently stored to MongoDB. Reading documents entailed listing all books and showing them on a website. Updating documents involved retrieving existing data, filling out a form, and saving the modified data back to MongoDB. Deleting documents entailed verifying the deletion and removing the document from the database.

We then moved on to a detailed demonstration and explanation of MongoDB's extensive querying features, including the ability to filter documents based on particular criteria and arrange query results by properties like publication date. The chapter looked deeper into MongoDB's aggregation mechanism, demonstrating how to count the number of books released annually. Additionally, text search capabilities was added, allowing users to look for books with specified keywords in their titles or summaries.

Overall, this chapter taught you how to successfully integrate and use MongoDB within a Django application, taking advantage of MongoDB's sophisticated querying and data management features to improve the BookTech application's functionality and speed.

Test Your Knowledge

1. What is a primary advantage of using NoSQL databases like MongoDB for web applications?

a) Fixed schema design
b) Complex SQL queries
c) Horizontal scalability
d) Limited data types

Answer: c) Horizontal scalability

2. Which library is used to connect Django to MongoDB?

a) django-mongodb
b) djongo
c) mongoengine
d) mongodjango

Answer: b) djongo

3. In the context of MongoDB, what does CRUD stand for?

a) Create, Read, Update, Delete
b) Create, Remove, Update, Drop
c) Create, Retrieve, Update, Drop
d) Create, Read, Upload, Delete

Answer: a) Create, Read, Update, Delete

4. Which Django model method is used to create a new document in MongoDB?

a) insert()
b) create()
c) save()
d) add()

Answer: b) create()

5. How do you filter documents based on specific criteria in Django using MongoDB?

a) Book.objects.query()
b) Book.objects.filter()
c) Book.objects.find()
d) Book.objects.search()

Answer: b) Book.objects.filter()

6. Which command is used to sort query results by a specific field in Django?

a) order_by()
b) sort_by()
c) filter_by()
d) arrange_by()

Answer: a) order_by()

7. What is the purpose of the __gt lookup in a Django query?

a) To group results
b) To filter results greater than a specified value
c) To search text fields
d) To join related models

Answer: b) To filter results greater than a specified value

8. How do you perform a text search on the title and summary fields in a MongoDB collection using Django?

a) Book.objects.filter(title__search=query, summary__search=query)
b) Book.objects.filter(Q(title__icontains=query) | Q(summary__icontains=query))
c) Book.objects.search(title=query, summary=query)
d) Book.objects.filter(text__search=query)

Answer: b) Book.objects.filter(Q(title__icontains=query) | Q(summary__icontains=query))

9. Which Django method is used to count the number of documents that match certain criteria?

a) count_documents()
b) count_objects()
c) aggregate()
d) count()

Answer: d) count()

10. What is the advantage of using MongoDB's aggregation framework?

a) Simplifies database migrations
b) Enables complex data processing and analytics
c) Provides automatic indexing
d) Improves database security

Answer: b) Enables complex data processing and analytics

CHAPTER 9: SITE MAPS, RSS FEEDS, AND SEO

Introduction

In this chapter, we will look at key features for improving the visibility and accessibility of your Django application. This chapter begins with the creation of site maps, which are an important tool for optimizing site navigation and assisting search engines in properly indexing your material. You'll discover how to design and customize site maps for your BookTech application. Next, we will look at how to set up RSS feeds, which are useful for sharing your information to a larger audience. This involves configuring Django to automatically generate RSS feeds, ensuring that your users are always up to current on the latest material.

We will go over some SEO (Search Engine Optimization) recommended practices to help your site rank higher in search results. These include ways to improve your site's structure and content so that search engines can more easily crawl and index it. We will also learn how to integrate Google Analytics into your Django site. This powerful tool offers insights into user behavior, allowing you to make data-driven decisions to boost user engagement and site performance.

The chapter is rounded up with a practical lab that allows you to integrate BookTech's analytics and search engine optimization capabilities. By using these concepts, you will ensure that your website is accessible, user-friendly, and search engine optimized, resulting in more traffic to your application.

Generating Site Maps

Overview

A site map is an XML file that lists the URLs of a website. It helps search engines like Google and Bing understand the structure of your site and index its content more efficiently. Creating a site map is an essential step for improving your website's SEO, ensuring all your pages are discoverable by search engines.

Essential Concepts

Change Frequency

The changefreq attribute in the sitemap classes specifies how often the content at a particular URL is likely to change. Common values include always, hourly, daily, weekly, monthly, yearly, and never.

Priority

The priority attribute indicates the priority of the URL relative to other URLs on your site. It ranges from 0.0 to 1.0, with 1.0 being the highest priority. This helps search engines determine the importance of the pages on your site.

Last Modified Date

The lastmod method returns the date when the content at the URL was last modified. This helps search engines know when to re-crawl the page.

Setting up Site Maps in Django

Install the Required Package

Django includes a built-in sitemap framework that makes generating site maps straightforward. Ensure the django.contrib.sitemaps application is included in your INSTALLED_APPS in settings.py:

```
INSTALLED_APPS = [

    ...

    'django.contrib.sitemaps',

    ...

]
```

Define a Sitemap Class

Create a sitemap class for your BookTech application. This class will specify which models should be included in the site map. For example, we will create a sitemap for the Book model.

Create a file named sitemaps.py in your library app directory:

```
from django.contrib.sitemaps import Sitemap

from .models import Book



class BookSitemap(Sitemap):

    changefreq = "weekly"

    priority = 0.8
```

```
    def items(self):
        return Book.objects.all()

    def lastmod(self, obj):
        return obj.publication_date
```

In the above given code snippet, the items method returns all the Book objects, and the lastmod method returns the publication date of each book, indicating when each book was last modified.

Configure the URL Configuration

Add the sitemap to your URL configuration. Update urls.py in your library app or the main urls.py file:

```
from django.contrib.sitemaps.views import sitemap
from django.urls import path
from .sitemaps import BookSitemap

sitemaps = {
    'books': BookSitemap,
}

urlpatterns = [
    ...
    path('sitemap.xml', sitemap, {'sitemaps': sitemaps},
name='django.contrib.sitemaps.views.sitemap'),
```

```
    ...
]
```

This configuration tells Django to generate a site map at http://yourdomain.com/sitemap.xml, containing the URLs specified in the BookSitemap class.

Customizing the Site Map

Customize your site map further by adding more models or filtering items. For instance, you can add an AuthorSitemap:

```
from django.contrib.sitemaps import Sitemap
from .models import Author


class AuthorSitemap(Sitemap):
    changefreq = "monthly"
    priority = 0.6


    def items(self):
        return Author.objects.all()


    def lastmod(self, obj):
        return obj.birth_date
```

Update your sitemaps dictionary in urls.py to include the new sitemap:

```
sitemaps = {
    'books': BookSitemap,
```

```
    'authors': AuthorSitemap,
}
```

Launch the Django development server and visit the URL http://127.0.0.1:8000/sitemap.xml. You should see an XML file listing the URLs of your book and author pages.

Adding Custom URLs to the Site Map

Sometimes, you may want to include URLs that are not directly tied to models. You can add custom URLs by extending the Sitemap class.

For example: Add a custom URL for the home page.

Create a Custom Sitemap Class

In sitemaps.py, add a custom sitemap class:

```
from django.urls import reverse
from django.contrib.sitemaps import Sitemap


class StaticViewSitemap(Sitemap):
    changefreq = "yearly"
    priority = 0.5


    def items(self):
        return ['home']


    def location(self, item):
        return reverse(item)
```

Update URL Configuration

Update the sitemaps dictionary in urls.py to include the new sitemap:

```
sitemaps = {

    'books': BookSitemap,

    'authors': AuthorSitemap,

    'static': StaticViewSitemap,

}
```

Restart the Django development server and check http://127.0.0.1:8000/sitemap.xml to see the custom URL included in the site map.

Handling Large Site Maps

If your site has a large number of URLs, you may need to split the site map into multiple files to manage the size. Django's sitemap framework handles this automatically by splitting the site map into separate index files.

For example: Adjust the number of items per sitemap file. In your BookSitemap class, set the limit attribute:

```
class BookSitemap(Sitemap):

    changefreq = "weekly"

    priority = 0.8

    limit = 500  # Number of items per sitemap file


    def items(self):

        return Book.objects.all()


    def lastmod(self, obj):
```

```
        return obj.publication_date
```

When the number of items exceeds the limit, Django will automatically create additional site map files. These site maps help search engines understand the structure of your site and index its content more effectively, improving your site's visibility and accessibility.

RSS Feeds

Introduction to RSS Feeds

RSS (Really Simple Syndication) feeds are a way to distribute content from your website to users who subscribe to the feed. An RSS feed is an XML file that lists recent content, such as blog posts, articles, or books, and allows users to stay updated with new content automatically. RSS feeds are essential for content distribution, enabling users to consume updates through feed readers or email subscriptions without visiting your site.

Setting up RSS Feeds

Install Required Package

Django has built-in support for creating RSS feeds. Ensure the django.contrib.syndication application is included in your INSTALLED_APPS in settings.py:

```
INSTALLED_APPS = [

    ...

    'django.contrib.syndication',

    ...

]
```

Create a Feed Class

Create a feed class for your BookTech application. This class will specify which models and fields should be included in the RSS feed. Create a file named feeds.py in your library app directory:

```
from django.contrib.syndication.views import Feed
```

```
from django.urls import reverse
from .models import Book


class LatestBooksFeed(Feed):
    title = "Latest Books"
    link = "/rss/"
    description = "Updates on the latest books in the
BookTech catalog."


    def items(self):
        return Book.objects.order_by('-
publication_date')[:5]


    def item_title(self, item):
        return item.title


    def item_description(self, item):
        return item.summary


    def item_link(self, item):
        return reverse('book_detail', args=[item.pk])
```

This class defines the RSS feed for the latest books, including the title, link, description, and the items to be included in the feed. The items method returns the latest five books ordered by publication date, and the item_title, item_description, and item_link methods define the title, description, and link for each item in the feed.

Configure the URL Configuration

Add the feed to your URL configuration. Update urls.py in your library app or the main urls.py file:

```
from django.urls import path

from .feeds import LatestBooksFeed


urlpatterns = [

    ...

    path('rss/', LatestBooksFeed(), name='rss_feed'),

    ...

]
```

This configuration tells Django to generate the RSS feed at http://yourdomain.com/rss/. And then as usual, go to the Django development server and visit the URL http://127.0.0.1:8000/rss/. You should see an XML file listing the latest books in the BookTech catalog.

Customizing the RSS Feed

Adding More Fields

You can include more fields in the RSS feed by overriding additional methods in your feed class. For example, add the author's name to the description:

```
def item_description(self, item):

    return f"{item.summary} (Author:
{item.author.first_name} {item.author.last_name})"
```

Including Author Information

To include detailed author information in the RSS feed, you might want to create a separate feed for authors. Update feeds.py:

```
from django.contrib.syndication.views import Feed

from .models import Author


class LatestAuthorsFeed(Feed):

    title = "Latest Authors"

    link = "/rss/authors/"

    description = "Updates on the latest authors in the
BookTech catalog."


    def items(self):

        return Author.objects.order_by('-birth_date')[:5]


    def item_title(self, item):

        return f"{item.first_name} {item.last_name}"


    def item_description(self, item):

        return f"Born on {item.birth_date}. Authored
books: {', '.join([book.title for book in
item.book_set.all()])}"
```

```
    def item_link(self, item):

        return reverse('author_detail', args=[item.pk])
```

Update the URL configuration to include the new feed:

```
urlpatterns += [

    path('rss/authors/', LatestAuthorsFeed(),
name='rss_authors_feed'),

]
```

Check http://127.0.0.1:8000/rss/authors/ to see the updated feed with author information.

Handling Media Content

If your items include media content, such as images or files, you can include these in the RSS feed using the item_enclosure_url and item_enclosure_length methods.

For example: Including book cover images in the RSS feed.

Add a Field for Book Cover Images

Ensure your book model includes a field for cover images:

```
from django.db import models



class Book(models.Model):

    ...

    cover_image = models.ImageField(upload_to='covers/',
blank=True, null=True)
```

Update the Feed Class

Update the LatestBooksFeed class to include the cover image:

```
def item_enclosure_url(self, item):
    return item.cover_image.url if item.cover_image else
''

def item_enclosure_length(self, item):
    return item.cover_image.size if item.cover_image else
0

def item_enclosure_mime_type(self, item):
    return 'image/jpeg'
```

Restart the server and check the RSS feed to see if the cover images are included.

SEO Best Practices

Key SEO Terms

Search Engine Optimization (SEO) is the process of improving the visibility and ranking of your website on search engines like Google. Effective SEO strategies ensure that your content is easily discoverable, which can lead to increased traffic and engagement.

Following are some key terms and concepts in SEO:

1. Keywords: Words or phrases that users type into search engines. Using relevant keywords in your content helps search engines understand the topic of your pages.
2. Meta Tags: HTML tags that provide metadata about your webpage. Important meta tags include the title tag and meta description.
3. Alt Text: Descriptions for images, helping search engines understand what the images depict.
4. Backlinks: Links from other websites to your site, which can improve your site's authority and ranking.
5. Content Quality: High-quality, relevant content is crucial for SEO. Search engines

prioritize content that provides value to users.

6. Mobile-Friendliness: Ensuring your site is optimized for mobile devices, as search engines favor mobile-friendly websites.
7. Site Speed: Fast-loading websites provide a better user experience and are favored by search engines.

Implementing SEO Best Practices

Using Relevant Keywords

Identify keywords related to your books and integrate them naturally into your content. For example, if you have a book on "Python Programming," use keywords like "learn Python," "Python tutorial," and "Python programming book" in the book's description and metadata.

Optimizing Meta Tags

Update your templates to include dynamic title tags and meta descriptions. For example, in your book_detail.html template:

```
<!DOCTYPE html>

<html>

<head>

    <title>{{ book.title }} - BookTech</title>

    <meta name="description" content="{{ book.summary
}}">

</head>

<body>

    <h1>{{ book.title }}</h1>

    <p>{{ book.summary }}</p>

    <!-- other content -->

</body>
```

```
</html>
```

This ensures each book's page has a unique title and description, improving its search engine visibility.

Adding Alt Text to Images

Ensure all images have descriptive alt text. Update your book model and template to include alt text for cover images:

```
<img src="{{ book.cover_image.url }}" alt="{{ book.title
}} cover image">
```

This helps search engines understand the content of your images and improves accessibility.

Creating High-Quality Content

Write detailed, informative descriptions for each book. Include relevant information like the author's background, the book's key topics, and any unique features. High-quality content is more likely to rank well in search results.

Improving Mobile-Friendliness

Ensure your BookTech site is responsive and works well on mobile devices. Use CSS frameworks like Bootstrap or implement responsive design techniques. For example:

```
<meta name="viewport" content="width=device-width,
initial-scale=1">
```

This tag ensures your site adjusts correctly on different screen sizes.

Enhancing Site Speed

Optimize your website's performance by compressing images, using efficient coding practices, and leveraging caching. For example, use Django's caching framework to cache frequently accessed data:

```
from django.core.cache import cache
```

```
def book_detail_view(request, book_id):
    book = cache.get(f'book_{book_id}')
    if not book:
        book = get_object_or_404(Book, id=book_id)
        cache.set(f'book_{book_id}', book, 300)  # Cache
for 5 minutes
    return render(request, 'library/book_detail.html',
{'book': book})
```

This reduces the load on your database and speeds up page loading times.

Generating a Sitemap

As learned in the previous section, ensure you have a sitemap set up for your site. This helps search engines crawl and index your content more effectively.

Integrating Social Sharing

Add social sharing buttons to your book detail pages. This encourages users to share your content, which can lead to more backlinks and improved search engine ranking. For example:

```
<div>
    <a
href="https://www.facebook.com/sharer/sharer.php?u={{
request.build_absolute_uri }}">Share on Facebook</a>
    <a href="https://twitter.com/intent/tweet?url={{
request.build_absolute_uri }}">Share on Twitter</a>
</div>
```

Implementing Structured Data

Use structured data to help search engines understand the content of your pages better. Implement JSON-LD for books. Add the following to your book_detail.html template:

```
<script type="application/ld+json">
{
    "@context": "http://schema.org",
    "@type": "Book",
    "name": "{{ book.title }}",
    "author": "{{ book.author.first_name }} {{
book.author.last_name }}",
    "datePublished": "{{ book.publication_date }}",
    "isbn": "{{ book.isbn }}",
    "description": "{{ book.summary }}",
    "image": "{{ book.cover_image.url }}"
}
</script>
```

This helps search engines display rich snippets for your books in search results.

Monitoring and Analyzing Performance

Use tools like Google Search Console to monitor your site's performance in search results. It provides insights into how Google indexes your site and identifies issues that need addressing.

Your books and other content will be much more visible in search engine results when you apply these SEO best practices. This will lead to more organic traffic, higher user engagement, and an increase in the reach and impact of your application.

Analytics Integration

Google Analytics is a powerful tool that provides insights into how users interact with your website. It helps you track various metrics such as page views, user demographics, traffic sources, and user behavior. Integrating Google Analytics into your BookTech application will enable you to make data-driven decisions to improve user engagement and overall site performance.

Setting up Google Analytics

Create a Google Analytics Account

If you don't already have a Google Analytics account, you'll need to create one. Go to Google Analytics site (https://analytics.google.com/) and sign in with your Google account. Follow the prompts to set up a new account for your BookTech application.

Setup a Property

In Google Analytics, a property represents your website. After creating your account, create a new property for BookTech. You'll be given a tracking ID (UA-XXXXXXXXX-X) and a tracking code snippet.

Install Google Analytics in Django

To integrate Google Analytics with your Django application, you'll need to add the tracking code to your HTML templates. This code snippet will send data to Google Analytics every time a user visits your site.

Open your main template file (e.g., base.html) and add the tracking code just before the closing </head> tag:

```
<!DOCTYPE html>

<html lang="en">

<head>

    <meta charset="UTF-8">

    <meta name="viewport" content="width=device-width,
initial-scale=1.0">

    <title>{% block title %}BookTech{% endblock
%}</title>

    {% block extra_head %}

    <!-- Google Analytics -->
```

```
    <script async
src="https://www.googletagmanager.com/gtag/js?id=UA-
XXXXXXXXX-X"></script>

    <script>

        window.dataLayer = window.dataLayer || [];

        function gtag(){dataLayer.push(arguments);}

        gtag('js', new Date());

        gtag('config', 'UA-XXXXXXXXX-X');

    </script>

    {% endblock %}

</head>

<body>

    {% block content %}{% endblock %}

</body>

</html>
```

Replace UA-XXXXXXXXX-X with your actual Google Analytics tracking ID.

To ensure Google Analytics is correctly installed, open your website in a browser and use the Google Tag Assistant (a Chrome extension) to check the implementation. Alternatively, you can verify in the Google Analytics real-time reports to see if your visit is being tracked.

Tracking Additional Events

Google Analytics can track more than just page views. You can also track user interactions, such as button clicks, form submissions, and downloads.

For example: Track a button click event. To do this, add a button to your template:

```
<button id="downloadButton">Download</button>
```

Add JavaScript to track the button click event:

```
<script>

document.getElementById('downloadButton').addEventListene
r('click', function() {
        gtag('event', 'click', {
            'event_category': 'button',
            'event_label': 'Download Button'
        });
    });
</script>
```

This code sends an event to Google Analytics every time the download button is clicked.

Hands-on Lab: Implement SEO and Analytics

Optimize Meta Tags and Content

Dynamic Meta Tags

Ensure each page has unique meta tags. Open your book_detail.html template and add the following meta tags:

```
<!DOCTYPE html>
<html>
<head>
    <title>{{ book.title }} - BookTech</title>
```

```
    <meta name="description" content="{{ book.summary
}}">

    <meta name="keywords" content="BookTech, {{
book.title }}, {{ book.author.first_name }} {{
book.author.last_name }}">

    <meta name="author" content="{{
book.author.first_name }} {{ book.author.last_name }}">

    <meta name="viewport" content="width=device-width,
initial-scale=1.0">

</head>

<body>

    <h1>{{ book.title }}</h1>

    <p>{{ book.summary }}</p>

    <!-- Other content -->

</body>

</html>
```

Alt Text for Images

Add descriptive alt text for images. Update your book_detail.html:

```
<img src="{{ book.cover_image.url }}" alt="{{ book.title
}} cover image">
```

Structured Data with JSON-LD

Implement structured data to help search engines understand your content better. Add the following JSON-LD script in book_detail.html:

```
<script type="application/ld+json">
```

```
{
    "@context": "http://schema.org",
    "@type": "Book",
    "name": "{{ book.title }}",
    "author": {
        "@type": "Person",
        "name": "{{ book.author.first_name }} {{
book.author.last_name }}"
    },
    "datePublished": "{{ book.publication_date }}",
    "isbn": "{{ book.isbn }}",
    "description": "{{ book.summary }}",
    "image": "{{ book.cover_image.url }}"
}
</script>
```

Add Social Sharing Buttons

Add Social Sharing Links

Enable users to share content on social media. Add sharing buttons to book_detail.html:

```
<div>
    <a
href="https://www.facebook.com/sharer/sharer.php?u={{
request.build_absolute_uri }}">Share on Facebook</a>
```

```
    <a href="https://twitter.com/intent/tweet?url={{
request.build_absolute_uri }}">Share on Twitter</a>

</div>
```

Integrate Google Analytics

Add Google Analytics Tracking Code

Integrate Google Analytics by adding the tracking code to base.html (or the main template used across all pages):

```
<!DOCTYPE html>

<html lang="en">

<head>

    <meta charset="UTF-8">

    <meta name="viewport" content="width=device-width,
initial-scale=1.0">

    <title>{% block title %}BookTech{% endblock
%}</title>

    {% block extra_head %}

    <!-- Google Analytics -->

    <script async
src="https://www.googletagmanager.com/gtag/js?id=UA-
XXXXXXXXX-X"></script>

    <script>

        window.dataLayer = window.dataLayer || [];

        function gtag(){dataLayer.push(arguments);}
```

```
        gtag('js', new Date());

        gtag('config', 'UA-XXXXXXXXX-X');

    </script>

    {% endblock %}

</head>

<body>

    {% block content %}{% endblock %}

</body>

</html>
```

Replace UA-XXXXXXXXX-X with your actual Google Analytics tracking ID.

Track Button Click Events

Track button clicks to measure user interactions. Add a download button and track its clicks in book_detail.html:

```
<button id="downloadButton">Download</button>

<script>

document.getElementById('downloadButton').addEventListene
r('click', function() {

        gtag('event', 'click', {

            'event_category': 'button',

            'event_label': 'Download Button'

        });
```

```
    });
</script>
```

Generate and Submit a Sitemap

Create Sitemap Class

In sitemaps.py, ensure your sitemap classes are defined:

```
from django.contrib.sitemaps import Sitemap
from .models import Book


class BookSitemap(Sitemap):
    changefreq = "weekly"
    priority = 0.8

    def items(self):
        return Book.objects.all()

    def lastmod(self, obj):
        return obj.publication_date
```

Configure URLs

Update your URL configuration in urls.py:

```
from django.contrib.sitemaps.views import sitemap
from .sitemaps import BookSitemap
```

```
sitemaps = {
    'books': BookSitemap,
}


urlpatterns = [
    path('sitemap.xml', sitemap, {'sitemaps': sitemaps}, name='sitemap'),
    ...
]
```

Launch the Django development server and visit the URL http://127.0.0.1:8000/sitemap.xml in your browser to verify your sitemap. Submit the URL to Google Search Console and Bing Webmaster Tools.

This hands-on practical exercise ensures your site is optimized for search engines and provides valuable insights into user behavior through Google Analytics. These enhancements will help you drive more traffic to your site, improve user engagement, and make data-driven decisions to enhance the overall effectiveness of your application.

Summary

To summarize, this chapter aimed to improve the visibility and accessibility of the BookTech application through SEO and analytics integration. The chapter began with explaining the necessity of creating site maps, which help search engines understand a website's structure and efficiently index its information. There were detailed instructions on making use of Django's in-built sitemap framework to design and modify site maps. The chapter then taught how to set up RSS feeds, which allow users to receive automatic updates on new information. This included developing feed classes and configuring URLs to generate RSS feeds for the most recent books and authors in the BookTech catalog.

We then taught you SEO best practices, covering topics like keywords, meta tags, alt text, backlinks, content quality, mobile friendliness, site speed, and structured data. We demonstrated how to add dynamic meta tags, informative alt text for photos, and structured data to our BookTech templates via JSON-LD. In addition, we included social sharing icons to facilitate content sharing on social networking networks. Google Analytics was then introduced wherein steps were provided for integrating Google Analytics into the BookTech application by adding the tracking code to the main template. Additionally, we showed how to set up goals in Google Analytics and how to track button clicks in greater detail.

Finally, the chapter closed with a hands-on lab in which all the above concepts were realistically tested. This included refining meta tags and content, integrating social sharing buttons, enabling Google Analytics tracking, creating and uploading a site map, and analyzing site performance using bespoke dashboards and automated reporting in Google Analytics. By taking this comprehensive strategy, we made sure that our BookTech application is search engine optimized and that it has robust analytics capabilities to boost user engagement and site efficacy.

Test Your Knowledge

1. What is the primary purpose of a site map in SEO?

a) To store user data
b) To help search engines understand the structure of your site
c) To enhance the site's visual appeal
d) To improve site speed

Answer: b) To help search engines understand the structure of your site

2. Which Django application provides built-in support for generating site maps?

a) django.contrib.sitemaps
b) django.contrib.rss
c) django.contrib.seo
d) django.contrib.analytics

Answer: a) django.contrib.sitemaps

3. What is an RSS feed used for?

a) To generate site maps
b) To distribute content updates automatically to users
c) To improve site speed
d) To track user interactions

Answer: b) To distribute content updates automatically to users

4. Which method in a Django RSS feed class returns the items to be included in the feed?

a) item_description()
b) item_title()

c) items()
d) item_link()

Answer: c) items()

5. What is the purpose of the meta description tag in SEO?

a) To set the viewport for mobile devices
b) To provide a summary of the page's content for search engines
c) To link to external CSS files
d) To specify the character encoding of the document

Answer: b) To provide a summary of the page's content for search engines

6. Which of the following is a key benefit of using structured data in SEO?

a) It increases the site's loading speed
b) It helps search engines display rich snippets in search results
c) It prevents search engines from indexing the site
d) It improves the site's design

Answer: b) It helps search engines display rich snippets in search results

7. What does the Google Analytics tracking code do when added to your website?

a) It speeds up the website
b) It tracks user interactions and sends data to Google Analytics
c) It generates site maps automatically
d) It blocks search engine crawlers

Answer: b) It tracks user interactions and sends data to Google Analytics

8. Where should the Google Analytics tracking code be placed in your HTML template?

a) At the bottom of the <body> tag
b) At the top of the <body> tag
c) Just before the closing </head> tag
d) Just after the opening <html> tag

Answer: c) Just before the closing </head> tag

9. How can you verify that Google Analytics is correctly installed on your site?

a) By checking the site's loading speed
b) By using the Google Tag Assistant or checking real-time reports in Google Analytics
c) By viewing the site's source code
d) By generating a site map

Answer: b) By using the Google Tag Assistant or checking real-time reports in Google Analytics

10. Which meta tag ensures that your site is mobile-friendly by setting the viewport?

a) <meta name="description" content="...">
b) <meta name="author" content="...">
c) <meta name="keywords" content="...">
d) <meta name="viewport" content="width=device-width, initial-scale=1.0">

Answer: d) <meta name="viewport" content="width=device-width, initial-scale=1.0">

CHAPTER 10: DEPLOYMENT AND SCALING

Introduction

In this chapter, we will go over the main processes for moving your BookTech application from development to production. This chapter starts with preparing your application for deployment, concentrating on best practices to ensure it's secure, efficient, and production-ready. We will look at how to containerize your Django application with Docker, which simplifies deployment and scaling by generating consistent environments.

Then, you'll get step-by-step instructions for deploying your application on popular cloud platforms such as AWS. These steps will teach you how to easily publish your app on online platforms. We will then introduce you to continuous integration and continuous deployment (CI/CD) pipelines, which allow for automatic testing and deployment of your application while ensuring new modifications are seamlessly incorporated into your production environment. Finally, we will learn maintenance and monitoring techniques to keep your application working smoothly and efficiently, as well as insights into techniques and tools for continuing management.

Preparing Deployment

As we reach the final stages of developing the BookTech application, we have successfully implemented core features and functionalities, including user authentication, CRUD operations for managing books, advanced querying with MongoDB, and real-time notifications with Django Channels. We've also enhanced the user experience with SEO optimization and integrated Google Analytics to monitor user interactions. It's time to prepare now the application for deployment, ensuring it is secure, efficient, and ready for a production environment.

Best Practices for Production Readiness

Environment Settings and Secrets Management

It's crucial to separate your development and production settings to avoid exposing sensitive information. Use environment variables to manage secrets like database credentials, API keys, and other sensitive data. For example, create a .env file for environment variables and use the django-environ package to load them in your settings.

```
DJANGO_SECRET_KEY=your-secret-key

DJANGO_DEBUG=False

DJANGO_ALLOWED_HOSTS=yourdomain.com
```

In settings.py, load these variables:

```
import environ

env = environ.Env()
environ.Env.read_env()

SECRET_KEY = env('DJANGO_SECRET_KEY')
DEBUG = env.bool('DJANGO_DEBUG', default=False)
ALLOWED_HOSTS = env.list('DJANGO_ALLOWED_HOSTS',
default=[])
```

Database Configuration

Ensure your database configuration is optimized for production. Use a production-ready database like PostgreSQL, which offers better performance and scalability compared to SQLite. For example, configure PostgreSQL in settings.py.

```
DATABASES = {
    'default': {
        'ENGINE': 'django.db.backends.postgresql',
        'NAME': env('DB_NAME'),
        'USER': env('DB_USER'),
        'PASSWORD': env('DB_PASSWORD'),
        'HOST': env('DB_HOST'),
        'PORT': env('DB_PORT'),
    }
```

```
}
```

Static and Media Files

Properly manage your static and media files. Use a CDN (Content Delivery Network) for serving static files and ensure media files are stored securely. For example, configure STATIC_URL and MEDIA_URL in settings.py.

```
STATIC_URL = '/static/'

MEDIA_URL = '/media/'


STATIC_ROOT = os.path.join(BASE_DIR, 'staticfiles')

MEDIA_ROOT = os.path.join(BASE_DIR, 'media')
```

Collect static files using the collectstatic command:

```
python manage.py collectstatic
```

Error Handling and Logging

Configure robust error handling and logging to monitor and troubleshoot issues in production. For example, setting up logging in settings.py.

```
LOGGING = {

    'version': 1,

    'disable_existing_loggers': False,

    'handlers': {

        'file': {

            'level': 'ERROR',

            'class': 'logging.FileHandler',
```

```
            'filename': os.path.join(BASE_DIR, 'logs',
'django_error.log'),

        },

        'console': {

            'class': 'logging.StreamHandler',

        },

    },

    'loggers': {

        'django': {

            'handlers': ['file', 'console'],

            'level': 'ERROR',

            'propagate': True,

        },

    },

}
```

Performance Optimization

Optimize your application's performance by implementing caching and database indexing. For example, to use Django's caching framework.

```
CACHES = {

    'default': {

        'BACKEND':
'django.core.cache.backends.memcached.MemcachedCache',
```

```
        'LOCATION': '127.0.0.1:11211',
    }
}
```

Ensure your database tables are indexed properly to speed up query performance.

These steps ensures your application is ready for a production environment. These practices will help maintain a reliable and scalable application in the production environment.

Docker and Django

Docker is a platform that allows you to develop, ship, and run applications in isolated environments called containers. Containers package an application and its dependencies, ensuring consistency across different environments, from development to production. Docker simplifies the deployment process, making it easier to manage and scale applications.

Installing Docker

Install Docker on Ubuntu

Update your package index and install necessary packages:

```
sudo apt-get update
sudo apt-get install \
    apt-transport-https \
    ca-certificates \
    curl \
    software-properties-common
```

Add Docker's official GPG key:

```
curl -fsSL https://download.docker.com/linux/ubuntu/gpg |
sudo apt-key add -
```

Add the Docker repository:

```
sudo add-apt-repository \
    "deb [arch=amd64]
https://download.docker.com/linux/ubuntu \
    $(lsb_release -cs) \
    stable"
```

Install Docker CE (Community Edition):

```
sudo apt-get update
sudo apt-get install docker-ce
```

Verify that Docker is installed correctly:

```
sudo docker run hello-world
```

Install Docker Compose

Docker Compose is a tool for defining and running multi-container Docker applications. Install Docker Compose by running:

```
sudo curl -L
"https://github.com/docker/compose/releases/download/1.29
.2/docker-compose-$(uname -s)-$(uname -m)" -o
/usr/local/bin/docker-compose
sudo chmod +x /usr/local/bin/docker-compose
docker-compose --version
```

Containerizing the BookTech

Create a Dockerfile

A Dockerfile contains instructions to build a Docker image for your application. Create a Dockerfile in the root of your BookTech project:

```
# Use the official Python image from the Docker Hub
FROM python:3.8-slim


# Set environment variables
ENV PYTHONDONTWRITEBYTECODE 1
ENV PYTHONUNBUFFERED 1


# Set work directory
WORKDIR /code


# Install dependencies
COPY requirements.txt /code/
RUN pip install --upgrade pip
RUN pip install -r requirements.txt


# Copy project
COPY . /code/
```

Create docker-compose.yml File

Docker Compose allows you to define and manage multi-container Docker applications. Create a docker-compose.yml file in the root of your project:

```yaml
version: '3.8'

services:
  db:
    image: postgres:13
    volumes:
      - postgres_data:/var/lib/postgresql/data
    environment:
      POSTGRES_DB: booktech
      POSTGRES_USER: user
      POSTGRES_PASSWORD: password

  web:
    build: .
    command: python manage.py runserver 0.0.0.0:8000
    volumes:
      - .:/code
    ports:
      - "8000:8000"
    depends_on:
      - db
```

```
volumes:
  postgres_data:
```

This file defines two services: db for the PostgreSQL database and web for the Django application.

Update Settings for Docker

Modify settings.py to use environment variables for database configuration. Add the following:

```
import os


DATABASES = {
    'default': {
        'ENGINE': 'django.db.backends.postgresql',
        'NAME': os.getenv('POSTGRES_DB'),
        'USER': os.getenv('POSTGRES_USER'),
        'PASSWORD': os.getenv('POSTGRES_PASSWORD'),
        'HOST': 'db',
        'PORT': 5432,
    }
}
```

Build and Run the Containers

Build and start your containers using Docker Compose:

```
docker-compose up --build
```

This command builds the Docker image and starts the containers. The application will be accessible at http://127.0.0.1:8000.

Migrate the Database

Run the database migrations to set up the PostgreSQL database:

```
docker-compose run web python manage.py migrate
```

Create a Django superuser to access the admin interface:

```
docker-compose run web python manage.py createsuperuser
```

Collect static files for the Django application:

```
docker-compose run web python manage.py collectstatic
```

You can access the Django admin interface at http://127.0.0.1:8000/admin using the superuser credentials you created.

Deploying with Docker Compose

Configure for Production

Update the docker-compose.yml file for a production environment. Adjust settings such as the number of replicas, logging, and network configurations. For example, adding replicas and logging:

```
version: '3.8'


services:

  db:

    image: postgres:13

    volumes:

      - postgres_data:/var/lib/postgresql/data
```

```
    environment:
      POSTGRES_DB: booktech
      POSTGRES_USER: user
      POSTGRES_PASSWORD: password

  web:
    build: .
    command: gunicorn BookTech.wsgi:application --bind
0.0.0.0:8000
    volumes:
      - .:/code
    ports:
      - "8000:8000"
    depends_on:
      - db
    deploy:
      replicas: 3
      resources:
        limits:
          cpus: "0.5"
          memory: 512M
      restart_policy:
```

```
        condition: on-failure
    logging:
      driver: "json-file"
      options:
        max-size: "200k"
        max-file: "10"

volumes:
  postgres_data:
```

Deploy to a Cloud Platform

Deploy the Dockerized application to a cloud platform such as AWS, Azure, or Google Cloud. Use services like Amazon ECS, Azure Kubernetes Service (AKS), or Google Kubernetes Engine (GKE) to manage your containers in production. For example, consider deploying to AWS ECS.

- Create an ECS cluster.
- Push your Docker image to Amazon ECR (Elastic Container Registry).
- Create a task definition and service in ECS to run your containers.

Following these steps and performing the entire process makes deployment easier and guarantees that the application runs consistently in different environments.

Deploying on AWS

AWS CodeDeploy is a fully managed deployment service that automates software deployments to a variety of compute services such as Amazon EC2, AWS Lambda, and on-premises servers. CodeDeploy helps ensure consistent application updates and avoids downtime during deployments.

Configuring AWS CodeDeploy

Setting up AWS CLI

First, install and configure the AWS CLI on your local machine to interact with AWS services.

```
sudo apt-get update

sudo apt-get install awscli
```

Configure AWS CLI

```
aws configure
```

Provide your AWS access key, secret key, region, and output format when prompted.

Launch EC2 Instances

Launch and configure EC2 instances that will host your Django application. Ensure the instances have IAM roles with the necessary permissions to access CodeDeploy and other AWS services.

- Go to the AWS Management Console, navigate to the EC2 dashboard, and launch an instance.
- Select an Amazon Machine Image (AMI), such as Amazon Linux 2.
- Choose an instance type, such as t2.micro for testing.
- Configure instance details, including IAM roles.
- Add storage and configure security groups to allow SSH and HTTP/HTTPS access.
- Launch the instance and connect to it via SSH.

Install CodeDeploy Agent on EC2

Connect to your EC2 instance and install the CodeDeploy agent:

```
sudo yum update -y

sudo yum install ruby

sudo yum install wget

cd /home/ec2-user

wget https://aws-codedeploy-us-east-1.s3.us-east-
1.amazonaws.com/latest/install
```

```
sudo chmod +x ./install

sudo ./install auto

sudo service codedeploy-agent start
```

Verify the agent is running:

```
sudo service codedeploy-agent status
```

Creating a CodeDeploy Application and Deployment Group

- Go to the AWS Management Console and navigate to the CodeDeploy dashboard. Click on "Create application."
- Enter an application name and choose "EC2/On-premises" as the compute platform. Click "Create application."
- In the CodeDeploy dashboard, select your application and click on "Create deployment group." Enter a deployment group name.
- Select the service role that grants CodeDeploy necessary permissions. Choose the EC2 instances by selecting tags or Auto Scaling groups.
- Configure deployment settings, including deployment type (e.g., In-place or Blue/Green). Click "Create deployment group."

Preparing Application for Deployment

- Create appspec.yml

The appspec.yml file defines the deployment actions for CodeDeploy. Create this file in your project root:

```
version: 0.0

os: linux

files:

  - source: /

    destination: /home/ec2-user/booktech
```

```
hooks:
  BeforeInstall:
    - location: scripts/before_install.sh
      runas: ec2-user
  AfterInstall:
    - location: scripts/after_install.sh
      runas: ec2-user
  ApplicationStart:
    - location: scripts/start_server.sh
      runas: ec2-user
  ApplicationStop:
    - location: scripts/stop_server.sh
      runas: ec2-user
```

- Create Deployment Scripts

Create a scripts directory in your project root and add the deployment scripts.

1. before_install.sh

```
#!/bin/bash
cd /home/ec2-user/booktech
sudo pip install -r requirements.txt
```

2. After_install.sh

```
#!/bin/bash
```

```
cd /home/ec2-user/booktech
python manage.py migrate
python manage.py collectstatic --noinput
```

3. start_server.sh

```
#!/bin/bash
cd /home/ec2-user/booktech
sudo systemctl start gunicorn
sudo systemctl enable gunicorn
```

4. stop_server.sh

```
#!/bin/bash
sudo systemctl stop gunicorn
```

Setting up Gunicorn and Nginx

Install and configure Gunicorn and Nginx on your EC2 instance to serve your Django application.

- Install Gunicorn

```
sudo pip install gunicorn
```

- Create Gunicorn Service

Create a Gunicorn service file in /etc/systemd/system/gunicorn.service:

```
[Unit]
Description=gunicorn daemon
After=network.target
[Service]
```

```
User=ec2-user

Group=nginx

WorkingDirectory=/home/ec2-user/booktech

ExecStart=/usr/local/bin/gunicorn --workers 3 --bind
unix:/home/ec2-user/booktech.sock
BookTech.wsgi:application


[Install]

WantedBy=multi-user.target
```

- Install and Configure Nginx

```
sudo amazon-linux-extras install nginx1

sudo systemctl start nginx

sudo systemctl enable nginx
```

- Configure Nginx

Create an Nginx configuration file for your application in /etc/nginx/conf.d/booktech.conf:

```
server {

    listen 80;

    server_name your_domain_or_IP;


    location = /favicon.ico { access_log off;
log_not_found off; }

    location /static/ {
```

```
        root /home/ec2-user/booktech;
    }

    location / {
        include proxy_params;
        proxy_pass http://unix:/home/ec2-
user/booktech.sock;
    }
}
```

- Test the Nginx configuration and restart the service:

```
sudo nginx -t
sudo systemctl restart nginx
```

Deploying the Application with CodeDeploy

- Zip Your Project Files

Zip your project files, including the appspec.yml and scripts directory:

```
zip -r booktech.zip *
```

- Upload the Zip File to S3
- Create a Deployment in CodeDeploy
    - In the CodeDeploy console, select your application and click on "Create deployment."
    - Choose the deployment group created earlier.
    - Select "My application is stored in Amazon S3."
    - Provide the S3 bucket name and object key for the zipped file.

    - Click "Create deployment."

- Monitor the deployment process in the CodeDeploy console. Once the deployment is complete, you can access your Django application via the public IP or domain name associated with your EC2 instance.

After completing these steps, your BookTech application has been deployed and AWS CodeDeploy has been configured. You can update your application efficiently and with minimal downtime thanks to this setup, which guarantees a seamless deployment process.

Continuous Integration

Jenkins Overview

Jenkins is an open-source automation server that enables continuous integration (CI) and continuous delivery (CD) for software development. It supports building, testing, and deploying applications, making it an excellent choice for managing CI/CD pipelines for Django applications. Jenkins is highly extensible with a vast library of plugins to integrate with various tools and platforms.

Setting up Jenkins for CI/CD

Install Jenkins

First, add Jenkins Repository and Key

```
wget -q -O - https://pkg.jenkins.io/debian/jenkins.io.key
| sudo apt-key add -

sudo sh -c 'echo deb http://pkg.jenkins.io/debian-stable
binary/ > /etc/apt/sources.list.d/jenkins.list'
```

Install Jenkins

```
sudo apt update

sudo apt install jenkins
```

Start Jenkins

```
sudo systemctl start jenkins
```

```
sudo systemctl enable jenkins
```

Open your browser and navigate to http://your_server_ip_or_domain:8080. You will be prompted to enter the initial admin password, which can be found using:

```
sudo cat /var/lib/jenkins/secrets/initialAdminPassword
```

Configure Jenkins

Follow the setup wizard to install suggested plugins and create an admin user. Then, install additional plugins needed for integrating with Git, Docker, and other tools by navigating to Manage Jenkins > Manage Plugins, and install the following plugins:

- Git Plugin
- Docker Pipeline Plugin
- Pipeline Plugin

Setup Jenkins Pipeline for BookTech

- Create a New Pipeline Job
    - Go to the Jenkins dashboard and click on "New Item."
    - Enter a name for your job, select "Pipeline," and click "OK."
- In the job configuration, scroll down to the "Pipeline" section and choose "Pipeline script from SCM." Configure the following:
    - SCM: Git
    - Repository URL: Enter the URL of your Git repository (e.g., https://github.com/yourusername/booktech.git).
    - Credentials: Add and select credentials if needed.
    - Branch Specifier: Specify the branch to build (e.g., */main).

Create a Jenkinsfile in the root of your repository with the following content:

```
pipeline {

    agent any
```

```
    environment {
        DOCKER_CREDENTIALS_ID = 'your-dockerhub-
credentials-id'
        DOCKER_IMAGE = 'your-dockerhub-username/booktech'
        DB_USER = 'your-db-user'
        DB_PASSWORD = 'your-db-password'
        DB_NAME = 'booktech'
    }

    stages {
        stage('Checkout') {
            steps {
                git branch: 'main', url:
'https://github.com/yourusername/booktech.git'
            }
        }

        stage('Build Docker Image') {
            steps {
                script {

docker.build("${DOCKER_IMAGE}:latest")
```

```
                }
            }
        }

        stage('Push Docker Image') {
            steps {
                script {

docker.withRegistry('https://index.docker.io/v1/',
"${DOCKER_CREDENTIALS_ID}") {

docker.image("${DOCKER_IMAGE}:latest").push()
                    }
                }
            }
        }

        stage('Deploy') {
            steps {
                sshagent(credentials: ['your-ssh-
credentials-id']) {
                    sh """
```

```
                    ssh -o StrictHostKeyChecking=no your-
ec2-user@your-ec2-ip '
                        docker pull
${DOCKER_IMAGE}:latest &&
                        docker stop booktech || true &&
                        docker rm booktech || true &&
                        docker run -d --name booktech -e
POSTGRES_DB=${DB_NAME} -e POSTGRES_USER=${DB_USER} -e
POSTGRES_PASSWORD=${DB_PASSWORD} -p 8000:8000
${DOCKER_IMAGE}:latest
                    '
                    """
                }
            }
        }

        stage('Migrate and Collect Static') {
            steps {
                sshagent(credentials: ['your-ssh-
credentials-id']) {
                    sh """
                    ssh -o StrictHostKeyChecking=no your-
ec2-user@your-ec2-ip '
```

```
                            docker exec booktech python
manage.py migrate &&
                            docker exec booktech python
manage.py collectstatic --noinput
                        '
                        """
                    }
                }
            }
        }

    post {
        always {
            cleanWs()
        }
    }
}
```

In the above pipeline script:

- environment: Sets environment variables for Docker credentials and database configurations.
- Checkout: Checks out the code from the Git repository.
- Build Docker Image: Builds the Docker image for the BookTech application.
- Push Docker Image: Pushes the Docker image to Docker Hub.
- Deploy: Pulls the latest Docker image on the EC2 instance, stops any existing container,

removes it, and runs the new container.

- Migrate and Collect Static: Executes database migrations and collects static files inside the running container.

Run the Pipeline

- Save the pipeline configuration and click "Build Now" to trigger the pipeline.
- Monitor the build process in the Jenkins console output.

Configure Webhooks

Set up a webhook in your Git repository to trigger Jenkins builds automatically on code changes.

- Go to your repository settings on GitHub.
- Navigate to "Webhooks" and click "Add webhook."
- Enter your Jenkins URL followed by /github-webhook/ (e.g., http://your-jenkins-url/github-webhook/).
- Select "Just the push event" and click "Add webhook."

You can rest assured that updates to your production environment will be consistent and reliable because this pipeline automates the process of building, testing, and deploying the application.

Maintenance and Monitoring

Once your BookTech application is deployed, it is essential to ensure its smooth operation and continuous performance. Maintenance involves regular updates, backups, and performance optimization, while monitoring allows you to detect issues early and respond promptly. In this section, we will explore tools and techniques to maintain and monitor your application effectively.

Monitoring Tools

Amazon CloudWatch

Amazon CloudWatch is a monitoring service for AWS cloud resources and applications. It provides data and actionable insights to monitor your applications, respond to system-wide performance changes, and optimize resource utilization.

In order to set up the CloudWatch:

- Navigate to the CloudWatch dashboard in the AWS Management Console.
- Configure metrics to monitor your EC2 instances, such as CPU utilization, memory usage, disk I/O, and network traffic.

- Set up alarms to notify you of any thresholds breaches, ensuring you can respond to issues promptly.

New Relic

New Relic offers application performance monitoring (APM) and infrastructure monitoring. It provides detailed insights into your application's performance and helps identify bottlenecks.

Similar to Amazon CloudWatch, in order to set up New Relic:

- Sign up for a New Relic account and create a new application.
- Install the New Relic Python agent in your Django application by adding it to requirements.txt and configuring it in your settings.

```
pip install newrelic
```

- Create a newrelic.ini configuration file and set the necessary configurations.
- Start your application with the New Relic agent:

```
NEW_RELIC_CONFIG_FILE=newrelic.ini newrelic-admin run-
program gunicorn BookTech.wsgi:application
```

Sentry

Sentry is an error tracking tool that helps developers monitor and fix crashes in real-time. It captures and reports errors, providing context to understand and resolve them quickly. To successfully setup the Sentry:

- Sign up for a Sentry account and create a new project.
- Install the Sentry SDK in your Django application:

```
pip install sentry-sdk
```

- Configure Sentry in your settings.py:

```
import sentry_sdk

from sentry_sdk.integrations.django import
DjangoIntegration
```

```
sentry_sdk.init(
    dsn="your-dsn-here",
    integrations=[DjangoIntegration()],
    traces_sample_rate=1.0,
    send_default_pii=True
)
```

Key Performance Indicators (KPIs)

Monitoring KPIs helps you keep track of your application's health and performance. Key KPIs to monitor include:

1. Response Time
   Measure the time it takes for your application to respond to user requests. Lower response times indicate better performance.
2. Error Rate
   Track the number and frequency of errors occurring in your application. A low error rate signifies a stable application.
3. Throughput
   Monitor the number of requests your application handles per minute. High throughput indicates your application can handle significant traffic.
4. CPU and Memory Usage
   Keep an eye on CPU and memory usage of your servers. High usage can indicate the need for scaling or performance optimization.
5. Database Performance
   Track query performance, connection times, and transaction rates. Efficient database performance is crucial for a responsive application.
6. Uptime
   Measure the amount of time your application is available and running. High uptime indicates reliability and stability.
7. User Engagement
   Monitor user engagement metrics such as active users, session duration, and user retention rates. High engagement indicates user satisfaction.

Sample Program

Configure CloudWatch Alarms

Set up alarms for critical metrics in CloudWatch to receive notifications when thresholds are breached. For example; setup an alarm for High CPU Utilization as below:

- Go to the CloudWatch dashboard and click on "Create Alarm."
- Select the EC2 instance you want to monitor.
- Choose the metric "CPUUtilization."
- Configure the alarm threshold (e.g., CPU utilization > 80%).
- Set up notification actions, such as sending an email or triggering an Auto Scaling action.

Automate Regular Tasks

Use cron jobs or AWS Lambda to automate regular maintenance tasks, such as backups and performance reports. Let us take an example of setting up a cron job for database backups as below:

- Create a script for taking database backups and saving them to S3.
- Set up a cron job to run the script periodically.

```
crontab -e
```

Add the cron job (e.g., run the script daily at midnight):

```
0 0 * * * /path/to/backup_script.sh
```

Use Monitoring Dashboards

Create dashboards in CloudWatch or New Relic to visualize your KPIs and get real-time insights into your application's performance. For example, create a CloudWatch dashboard as per below steps:

- Go to the CloudWatch dashboard and click on "Create Dashboard."
- Add widgets for key metrics, such as CPU utilization, memory usage, and response times.
- Arrange the widgets to create a comprehensive view of your application's health.

Your BookTech application's continued health and performance can be guaranteed by employing these above strategies for continued maintenance and monitoring. You can keep your app running smoothly and reliably by updating it often, monitoring it for potential issues, and optimizing its performance.

Summary

In this final chapter, we made sure the BookTech application would work properly in a production setting by deploying and scaling it. The chapter began with configuring the application for deployment, emphasizing the necessity of separating development and production settings, securing environment variables, optimizing database setups, and handling static and media files. It also discussed security methods such using HTTPS, configuring secure HTTP headers, and ensuring correct error handling and logging.

The following section explained Docker and how to containerize the BookTech application. This involved making a Dockerfile and a docker-compose.yml file, configuring Django settings for Docker, and generating and running Docker containers. We went over each step of utilizing AWS CodeDeploy to deploy the app to AWS. This included deploying the CodeDeploy agent on EC2 instances, establishing a CodeDeploy application and deployment group, and configuring deployment scripts. The CodeDeploy deployment process ensured that deployments were automated and reliable. Continuous integration and continuous delivery (CI/CD) were next addressed, with Jenkins being introduced as the chosen tool. Jenkins was activated for the BookTech app by establishing a Jenkins pipeline, configuring Jenkins to build and deploy the app, and establishing webhooks to trigger automatic builds in response to code changes.

The chapter wrapped off with methods for monitoring and maintenance to ensure the application runs well. Key performance indicators (KPIs) like response time, error rate, throughput, and resource usage were identified along with regular maintenance tasks like backups, updates, and performance optimization. Tools like Amazon CloudWatch, New Relic, and Sentry were explored for monitoring performance and errors. These techniques ensure that the BookTech application remains stable, safe, and efficient in a production setting.

Test Your Knowledge

1. Why is it important to separate development and production settings in a Django application?

a) To improve site speed
b) To enhance user interface design
c) To avoid exposing sensitive information
d) To enable debugging in production

Answer: c) To avoid exposing sensitive information

2. Which file in a Docker project defines the instructions to build a Docker image?

a) docker-compose.yml
b) requirements.txt
c) settings.py
d) Dockerfile

Answer: d) Dockerfile

3. What is the purpose of the docker-compose.yml file?

a) To define environment variables
b) To install Python packages
c) To manage multi-container Docker applications
d) To configure Django settings

Answer: c) To manage multi-container Docker applications

4. Which AWS service automates software deployments to various compute services?

a) AWS CloudWatch
b) AWS CodeDeploy
c) AWS Lambda
d) AWS S3

Answer: b) AWS CodeDeploy

5. In AWS CodeDeploy, what is the appspec.yml file used for?

a) To store application logs
b) To define deployment actions and hooks
c) To configure database settings
d) To manage EC2 instance types

Answer: b) To define deployment actions and hooks

6. What is the main role of Jenkins in CI/CD pipelines?

a) To serve static files
b) To automate testing and deployment processes
c) To provide database backups
d) To monitor application performance

Answer: b) To automate testing and deployment processes

7. Which plugin is essential for Jenkins to interact with Git repositories?

a) Docker Pipeline Plugin
b) Git Plugin
c) Pipeline Plugin
d) Sentry Plugin

Answer: b) Git Plugin

8. What is a key benefit of using Docker for deploying applications?

a) Improved application aesthetics
b) Consistency across different environments
c) Enhanced debugging capabilities
d) Reduced need for testing

Answer: b) Consistency across different environments

9. Which of the following is NOT a key performance indicator (KPI) for monitoring application health?

a) Response Time
b) Error Rate
c) User Interface Design
d) CPU and Memory Usage

Answer: c) User Interface Design

10. Which monitoring tool provides real-time error tracking for Django applications?

a) AWS CloudWatch
b) New Relic
c) Sentry
d) Jenkins

Answer: c) Sentry

Index

L

M

N

O

P

Q

R

S

T

U

V

W

X

Epilogue

With this, I hope that you have gained the confidence and knowledge to build scalable web applications as we wrap up our journey together. Looking back on our journey together, it's obvious that you've accomplished a lot, becoming an expert in the fundamentals and advanced features of this robust framework.

We started by making our BookTech project and establishing our development environment. The success of the subsequent tasks depended on this first stage. By learning how to set up virtual environments and comprehend the project structure, you were able to lay the groundwork for organized and efficient development.

As a next major step, we implemented Django models and object relationship management. You confidently dove into managing database migrations, executing complicated queries, and defining models. With these abilities, you can interact with data in a natural and efficient way, which is essential for any Django application. Your applications are now powerful and efficient, thanks to your newfound confidence in handling database interactions.

Going ahead, you have a firm grasp on URL routing and views. You learned to handle requests and render responses with precision, whether it was function-based views or class-based views. You became an expert at mapping URLs to views and managing forms within views, which greatly improved your capacity to build interactive and dynamic web applications. It was just as satisfying to go through the templates. You learned about template inheritance, tags, and filters, and you experimented with making and customizing templates. A fantastic user experience was guaranteed by making sure your web pages were responsive and dynamic by passing context to templates.

Ensuring user authentication and authorization were key components of our study. You managed permissions, user registration, and login in a secure way. You could customize your application's user experience to fit specific needs by extending the default user model. This way, you could ensure both functionality and security. We also learned about visibility and search engine optimization, which involves making your site friendlier to search engines. You improved your app's discoverability and user engagement by making site maps, establishing RSS feeds, and using search engine optimization best practices. To succeed in today's cutthroat online environment, these abilities are must-haves.

The difficulties of deployment and scaling weren't going to stop you. Your deployments were consistent, reliable, and efficient because you used Docker to containerize your application, AWS for deployment, and Jenkins for CI/CD pipeline setup. Keeping production settings at a high standard requires these methods, which are priceless. At last, you realized how to keep your app running smoothly by utilizing monitoring and maintenance tools such as Sentry, Amazon CloudWatch, and New Relic. You can keep your application running smoothly and fix any problems that come up fast by monitoring performance metrics and error logs.

As we wrap up this book, keep in mind that what you've learned is only the tip of the iceberg. I hope you'll keep delving into Django 5, as it's a robust framework with limitless potential. Thanks to Django 5, you'll be able to keep up with the constantly changing web development landscape. I appreciate you sticking with me as we cover "Learning Django 5." It is my sincere wish that this book has served as a source of both practical knowledge about Django and motivation to explore new frontiers in web development. Continue to code, keep learning, and make incredible apps. I am excited to see what you create next because the world of web development is at your fingertips.

Thank You

www.ingramcontent.com/pod-product-compliance
Lightning Source LLC
Chambersburg PA
CBHW080209170726
48282CB00030B/1048
9788119177820